CIA

CATALOG OF CLANDESTINE WEAPONS, TOOLS, AND GADGETS

D1105975

Property of
The Public Library of Nashville and Davidson County
225 Polk Ave., Nashville, Tn. 37203

DISCARDED

CIA

CATALOG OF CLANDESTINE WEAPONS, TOOLS, AND GADGETS

JOHN MINNERY

Barricade Books Inc.
Fort Lee, New Jersey

Also by John Minnery:

How To Kill, Volumes I - VI
Pick Guns: Lock Picking For Spies, Cops, and Locksmiths
Fingertip Firepower: Pen Guns, Knives, and Bombs

Neither the author nor the publisher assumes any responsibility
for the use or misuse of information contained in this book.

Published by Barricade Books Inc.
1530 Palisade Avenue, Fort Lee, NJ 07024
by agreement with Paladin Press

Distributed by Publishers Group West
4065 Hollis, Emeryville, CA 94608

Copyright © 1990 by John Minnery

All rights reserved.

No part of this book may be reproduced, stored in a retrieval system,
or transmitted in any form, by any means, including mechanical,
electronic, photocopying, recording, or otherwise,
without the prior written permission of the publisher, except by
a reviewer who wishes to quote brief passages in connection
with a review written for inclusion in a magazine,
newspaper, or broadcast.

Printed in the United States of America.

Library of Congress Cataloging-in-Publication Data

Minnery, John.
  The CIA catalog of clandestine weapons, tools, and gadgets / John
Minnery.
  ISBN 0-942637-69-0; $9.95
1. Weapons—United States—Catalogs. 2. Tools—United States—
Catalogs. 3. United States. Central Intelligence Agency—Equipment
and supplies—Catalogs. I. Title.
U818.M56 1992
355.8'24—dc20   92-15887
                                                    CIP

CONTENTS

ACKNOWLEDGMENTS

would like to credit my friends and associates who have been of great assistance in the preparation of this book.

Mr. Keith Melton, curator, Clandestine Services Museum (private), allowed me to view and record his outstanding collection of espionage equipment gathered from around the world. That collection formed the bedrock of this catalog, and without the kind assistance of Mr. Melton, this work would not have been possible. Thanks also to Mr. Willi Krauss, Acton, Ontario; Mr. Jack Krcma, Toronto, Ontario; Mr. Elliot Riggs, Farmington, New Mexico; and Mr. Chris Schram, Art-Ex, Brantford, Ontario.

INTRODUCTION

his catalog of CIA E&E (Escape and Evasion) devices is a synthesis of the actual order book used by CIA personnel in the field to send for items they needed to insure their safety during a mission or to assist them in fleeing from apprehension if discovered or escaping from custody if captured.

CIA has been operating abroad for more than thirty years, and the purpose of this listing is to present a historical snapshot of devices included in its catalog during that time. Some items are from the early days after World War II, when there were stocks left over from the Office of Strategic Services (OSS). Others are from escape kits prepackaged by the British Special Operations Executive (SOE) and the escapes division of Military Intelligence (MI9) for Allied agents and aircrews who were trapped behind enemy lines. As the Cold War progressed, new devices were added to the catalog as old gadgets were "blown," or became known to adversaries of the United States. Technological advances and miniaturization also allowed certain items to be

CIA's Technical Services Division (TSD) Building, where the research and development of E&E catalog items takes place.

consolidated, expanded, or eliminated from the catalog.

CIA operations on a world scale required the warehousing of stockpiles of these devices on every continent so that they could be supplied without delay. These Quartermaster intelligence stores also had to inventory and update their stocks regularly. (Incidentally, the "Q" that supplies James Bond with his gadgets stands for Quartermaster.) Some specialty items had to be ordered from the Langley, Virginia, CIA headquarters (code-named KURIOT).

In compiling this catalog, the numbering sequence of the original CIA catalogs has been preserved where possible, as have the descriptions and technical specifications. My own comments and observations immediately follow the official text. The information on silenced and special weapons at the beginning of this book was taken directly from CIA Technical Services Division (TSD) documents published in October 1965. (In spite of this, CIA adamantly denies the existence of such weapons.) It was included because of its close relationship to the E&E catalog items upon which this book is based.

The photographs included in the original catalog

were not of very high quality. Items were wired to a board, and "white-out" was used to define them against this background. Further enhancement was necessary for this study, and the photos and illustrations included represent the best available renderings. In some photos, the reader will note a black oblong, which represents a one-inch scale for reference.

E&E devices are but a small part of CIA's global effort to be of service to those brave souls who search and listen for the "truth that makes us free." This work is a history; not an exposé. Items unknown to adversaries remain so.

SPECIAL WEAPONS

ithin the intelligence community, there exists the capability of developing and producing special weapons that may be adapted readily for concealment. Depending upon their intended use, they may be in a variety of sizes, have different lethality, and be silenced or unsilenced.

A brief description of special weapons currently available may be found on the following page.

Silenced and Special Weapons Under TSD Cognizance

.22-caliber stinger	*stock*
.22-caliber high-standard pistol, silenced	*stock*
.22-caliber high-standard pistol with interchangeable, silenced barrel	*development*
.22-caliber high-standard pistol with scope and stock	*prototype*
.22-caliber Browning rifle, silenced	*prototype*
7.65mm Walther PPK pistol with muzzle silencer	*ad hoc*
9mm Dear weapon	*stock*
9mm Welrod	*stock*
9mm silenced sidearm	*development*
9mm Gustaf SMG, silenced	*prototype*
9mm telecartridge rounds (silenced)	*development*
.38-caliber silenced rounds	*special issue*
.45-caliber M3 SMG with silenced barrel	*stock*
.45-caliber M-70 Winchester, silenced	*ad hoc*
.303-caliber Enfield rifle, silenced	*experimental*
Crossbow	*development*

Item 1: Pistol, 9mm (Dear Weapon)

Parabellum, single shot, 2-in. barrel, reloadable, c/w 3 cartridges in grip, packed for air drop. Expendable. Ref. 1395-H00-9108.

This pistol is now generally referred to as the Deer Gun. CIA lists it as the "Dear Weapon," which has an entirely different connotation, although both terms serve to disguise its use.

In the early 1970s it was called the "CIA Zip Gun" and was produced for use behind lines in counter-insurgency missions. It is the successor to the FP .45 "Liberator" pistol that was used for similar purposes during World War II. OSS referred to it as "The

bắn súng

This illustration, from a CIA Vietnamese language instruction manual, depicts the shooting of a Vietcong cadre member with the Dear Weapon.

Woolworth Gun" in their literature, referring to its cheap, throwaway nature. The Dear Weapon continued this tradition. It came packaged in a Styrofoam box so it could be dropped "as is" from a plane and would float. Inside the box was the weapon, three cartridges of ammunition, and a small, moisture-resistant instruction manual in pictogram or cartoon form so that it required no translation (although those dropped in Vietnam did have instructions in Vietnamese written beneath the drawings). The ammo could be stored inside the hollow grip by means of a rubber grip plug. The barrels were generally smooth-bore, although rifled ones exist in some collections (perhaps as a result of Bureau of Alcohol, Tobacco and Firearms [BATF] strictures against smooth-bore pistols). The screw-barrel design permitted different calibers and barrel lengths when warranted. Many thousands of these pistols were destroyed after the Vietnam War, and only a handful still exist outside CIA.

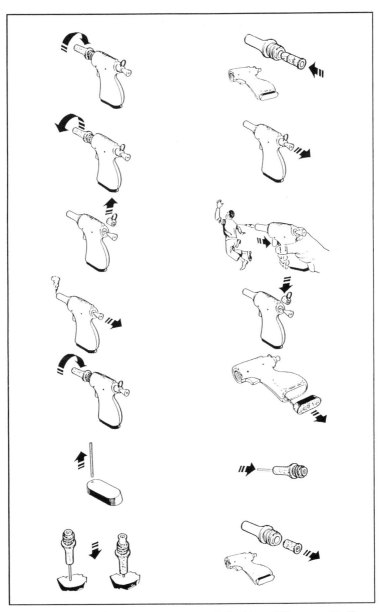

The loading and firing sequence of the Dear Weapon. Follow left to right, top to bottom. (Illustration courtesy of Elliot Riggs.)

Item 2: Stinger, .22-Caliber

Reloadable; c/w 7 cartridges, spare barrel, in lead foil tube. Expendable. Ref. 1395-H00-0069.

This diminutive weapon is made chiefly of machined aluminum alloy and is somewhat unique in that the barrel is not bored all the way through. The barrel is blown through upon discharging the weapon. This serves to seal the bore from dirt and to disguise the weapon somewhat, since no offending muzzle is visible.

The Stinger may be hidden inside a toothpaste or similar type of tube. It comes with seven (sometimes eight) .22 Long cartridges arranged within a clear plastic collar that unites the weapon with the spare barrel for storage. It can be easily hidden under the armpits or between the legs, and it can be taped in unlikely search locations. Some configurations allow it to be hidden internally.

The term "Stinger" harkens back to the .22 Short pen gun, Stinger T-2, issued to OSS during World War II as a hideout weapon and used to prevent capture by shooting at close range into the face of a potential captor. It could kill, but the goal was to startle and confuse an enemy long enough to undertake some follow-up action in conjunction with the firing of the round. (When these weapons were dropped to Kachin tribesmen in the remote jungles of Burma, the Kachin did not understand their use, but they had great fun "stinging" each other's bare anatomies, consequently inflicting more casualties upon themselves than on the Japanese!)

The weapon was originally a CIA design, but it was produced later by Military Armaments Corp. (the same firm that produced the Ingram MAC 10 submachine gun) and sold commercially as the "Single-Shot Survival Weapon" (SSSW-l). For a complete history, see

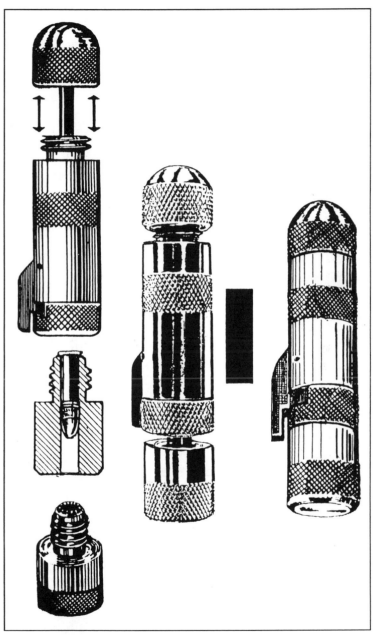

The loading sequence of the Stinger. (Author illustration.)

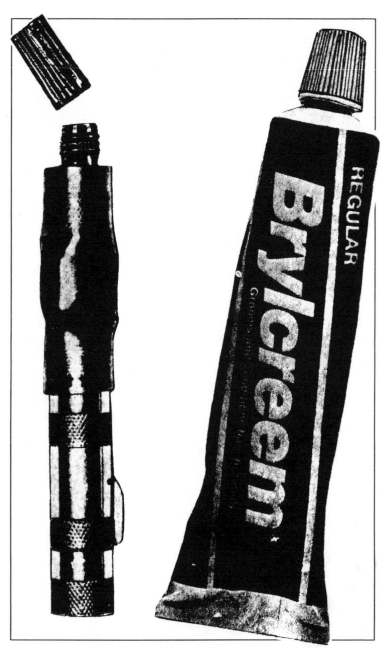

The Stinger in transit. (Author illustration.)

The Stinger complete with spare barrel and tube of ammunition. (Photo courtesy of Keith Melton.)

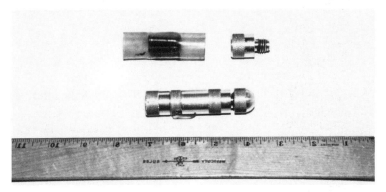

Stinger kit showing spare barrel, cartridge tube junction, and the assembled weapon. (Photo courtesy of Keith Melton.)

my book entitled *Fingertip Firepower: Pen Guns, Knives, and Bombs*, also published by Paladin Press.

Item 3: Camouflaged Weapon, .22-Caliber

Single shot, already loaded and not reloadable. Fires 40-grain .22-caliber bullet. Barrel length, 1 1/4 in.; overall length, 2 3/4 in.; powder charge, 50 mg. Bullseye powder; muzzle velocity, 759 fps; penetration, 1 3/4 in. in soft pine; operating temperature, 0-160 F; safety, wire-pull; range, max. 10 ft. Camouflaged as a popular brand of European king-size cigarette. E&E. Expendable. Ref. 1395-HOO-5670.

The camouflaged .22-caliber weapon is intended for use only as an escape aid when the captive must place his or her chances of escape on firing one shot. It is intended for use at close ranges, varying from actual contact to eight feet. There is sufficient muzzle energy to inflict a lethal wound with a well-placed hit. Only one shot is available, so that shot must be used to the best advantage.

The weapon is intended to recoil out of the operative's hand in a safe direction rather than forcing him or her to try to absorb the recoil by taking a good grip, as one would with a pistol (see accompanying illustration and instruction sheet). This same technique was advocated in the firing of SOE pen pistols during World War II.

I once had a cigarette pistol that was loaded and armed when a visitor noticed it on a desk and proceeded to pick it up and examine it before I could call out a warning. The visitor triggered it, but fortunately for all concerned, it misfired because its spring had weakened as a result of its being permanently cocked and compressed for many years! Upon seeing it misfire, I remained prayerfully quiet, and the visitor never knew the danger of the camouflaged pistol he had held.

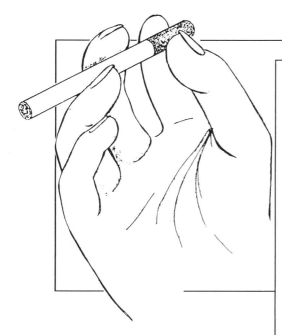

CIA illustration and instructions for the cigarette camouflaged weapon.

OPERATING INSTRUCTIONS

1. Hold the item as shown in the sketch.

2. Pull safety pin out with your left hand or with your teeth.

3. With the thumb and forefinger, rotate the end *counterclockwise* as far as it will go. The item is now armed and ready to fire.

4. Hold the item so that the end, between your thumb and forefinger, is NOT in line with your body. Push forward with your thumb and forefinger to fire.

CAUTION:

Observe the following precautions to prevent injury to yourself: When fired, the item will recoil out of your hand, but if it is directed away from your body, no injury or discomfort will result. Be sure to hold the item as shown and do not put your thumb over the end to push for firing.

Item 4: Concealable Weapon, .22-Caliber

Single shot, already loaded and not reloadable. Various barrel lengths: 1 1/4; 3; 4 3/4; and 5 in. Powder charge, 70 mg. Bullseye powder; operating temperature, 0-160 degrees Fahrenheit; safety, wire-pull; range, more than 10 ft. Longer barrels produce slightly greater muzzle energies and must be concealed in larger items. Operatives are to provide personal effects for this purpose or specify concealment types desired, such as pen, pencil, wallet, etc. E&E. Expendable. Ref. 1395-H00-5671.

Personal effects sent in for modification into weapons might include pocket flashlights; pocket-size books such as address books, diaries, or Bibles; pipes; cigarette cases; or similar portable items habitually carried by the operative.

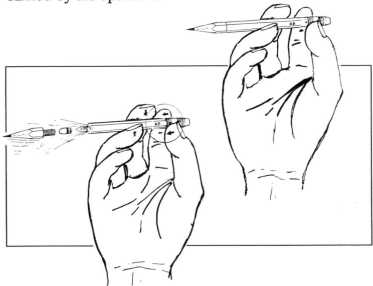

The technique for holding and firing the pencil concealable weapon. (Author illustration.)

The pencil pistol is fired much the same way as the camouflaged cigarette weapon, only it is harder hitting and has a longer range, making it more important to take provisions to accommodate recoil. Pistols built into heavier, longer items are more stable to fire when hand-held and can sometimes be aimed and fired accurately up to thirty feet with practice. (Practice is not always a luxury the average operative enjoys, and it is not the use for which the weapon is intended; still, it's comforting to know that the potential is there.)

Like "L" pills (lethal tablets of cyanide), these pistols may be used as instruments of suicide if escape is patently unlikely. (This is not recommended officially, but left to the individual conscience of the operative. The operative knows what may be revealed and the lives that might depend upon his or her silence. The approved technique is to shoot oneself in the mouth or throat so as to make it physically impossible to speak for days at the very least.)

Item 5: Explosive Cartridge, .45-Caliber

Single cartridge; no. 1 grade; approximately 173 grain weight. Muzzle velocity, 1140 fps with 5-in. barrel. Fits any weapon chambered for .45-caliber (U.S. 1911 case). Contains bullet that detonates approximately .006 seconds after impact. Packed 5 per tear-strip can. Expendable. Ref. 1305-H00-4405.

More than 100 years ago, Lt. Col. George V. Fosbery, V.C., designed and manufactured explosive bullets and equipped a company of his marksmen with them. The men went into action on the Northwest Frontier of India and employed their bullets as ranging or spotting rounds to judge the accuracy of their fire. They also used them to blow up the enemy ammunition limbers, although antipersonnel use was of secondary importance. (Fosbery also invented the Webley-Fosbery automatic revolver, but his first design was based on the Colt .45 Model 1873 "Bisley.")

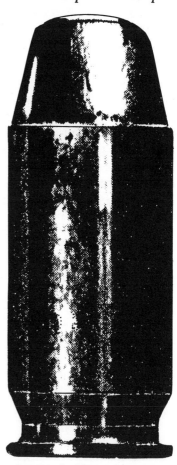

The exploding .45 auto cartridge. (Author illustration.)

Exploding bullets became commercially available in the 1970s, but they were found to be less lethal than standard .22-caliber cartridges because of poor penetration. (They often disintegrated before reaching vital structures.) Also, the space hollowed out to hold the primer and gunpowder took away from the weight of the original bullet. The rounds would misfire when penetrating flesh and fatty areas, and they would sometimes squib, or "jet," rather than explode when coming into contact with bone. (This is what saved President Reagan when he was shot in the armpit with a ".22 Exploder Bullet.")

CIA's explosive-type rounds have a built-in time delay, which allows deeper penetration. Its .22-caliber version explodes via an internal fuze, whether the round impacts a bony surface or not, and it does enhance lethality. It can also be used for spotting or exploding gasoline, and so forth. As an added advantage, obliterated rounds cannot be traced.

Item 6: Silenced Cartridge, .38-Caliber

This unique round was an outgrowth of research that began during the Vietnam War to assist the U.S. Army in arming the "tunnel rats" (men of short stature whose unenviable task it was to go down into the Vietcong tunnels and ferret out the enemy). Since firing regular ammo underground would momentarily deafen and blind the shooters, they needed a silent, flashless weapon. Silencers were tried but proved unsuitable. A quiet, special-purpose round was developed and shipped over for testing. The round fired a type of shot load that misfired due to improper primer seating, and it received a negative evaluation.

CIA recognized the merits of the round, however, and developed this silenced cartridge, which fires a .38 bullet (prior to this, it had been virtually impossible to fire a revolver silently).

Based on the captive piston principle, the round acts as a miniature engine. With but one stroke, it impels the bullet down the barrel at high speed, and yet contains all the forces of explosive combustion within the shell casing. The stainless-steel casing is, of necessity, thicker than a regular round, and the primer is also shrouded and held in place by a rear bulkhead or threaded end cap. The piston is checked in its forward motion by a machined shoulder that slams against a corresponding neck within the round and effectively seals the gasses; hence, it is rendered both noiseless and flashless.

Although it is not recommended, it is possible to reload this type of round. There is no telltale smell of smoke after firing this round, and when it is fired from a disguised weapon, no one but the victim is any the wiser. It is best used at close combat ranges of up to thirty feet. The .38-caliber silenced cartridge is

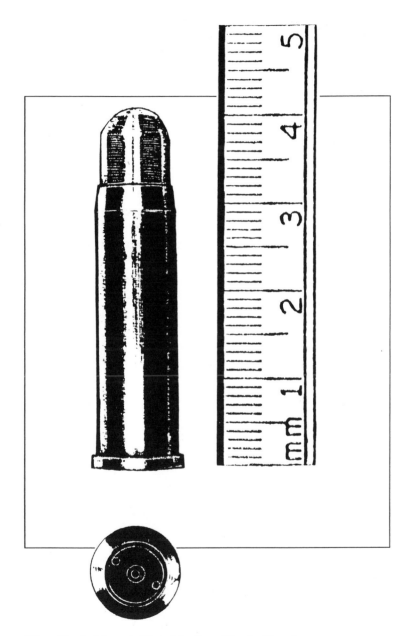

The silent .38 cartridge. (Author illustration.)

unrivaled for taking
out a border sentry or
a guard dog. Six shots
in the dark give new
significance to the
"dog who didn't bark
in the night."

**This field-reloadable
silent 30-gauge car-
tridge is custom-built.
The captive piston seen
extending from the
cartridge case pushes
the aluminum pro-
jectile. The assembled
round lies alongside it
(right).**

Item 7: Lock-Pick Knife

The jackknife, with its provision of many folding blades, is a natural housing for a selection of lock-picking instruments. Given that CIA is required to operate in so many diverse locales, it has attempted to provide a universal range of lock-picking tool "blades." The skeleton key and associated lever-lock hook probes are more common in Europe, while the pin-tumbler sinusoidal or wavy picks are predominant in countries served by North American hardware (which might also include regions of Asia). In most countries, both types of locks may be found. Many foreign cars have wafer-tumbler locks.

All but the most elementary warded-type locks require that a tension wrench (or more correctly, a torque wrench) be used in conjunction with the pick. This is an L-shaped spring-steel strip that applies rotational direction on the central turning plug of the lock. In lever locks, the levers are then lifted until their gates line up with a stump on the bolt, allowing the lock to be opened. In pin-tumbler locks, the two-part

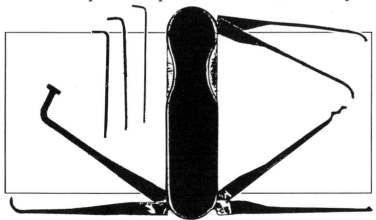

The lock-pick knife has a variety of extended picks, complete with three tension wrenches. (Illustration courtesy of Keith Melton.)

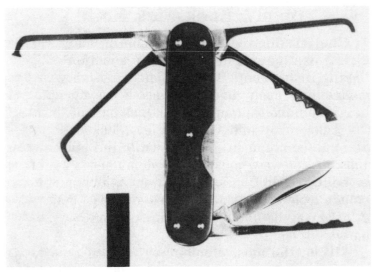

OSS lock-pick knife. (Photo courtesy of Keith Melton.)

pins are raised until their joints line up with the plug circumference, called the "shear line." When all the pins are aligned at that shear line, the lock is free to turn.

There is more to it than this brief explanation conveys, of course, and the very fact that picking is at all possible has a great deal to do with mechanical tolerances and a deft balancing of pressures applied and coordinated to lift the tumblers and turn the plug. Lock picking is an acquired mechanical skill that improves proportionately with the amount of practice undertaken. Getting in or out requires a modicum of familiarity with lock internals. Not all locks respond to manipulation, no matter how skilled the operative. Alternative entries and bypasses must also be learned. CIA TSD personnel will fly anywhere to open locks and provide keys for operatives who require assistance.

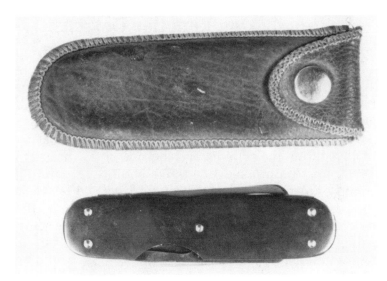

Folded lock-pick knife complete with carrying case. (Photo courtesy of Keith Melton.)

Item 8: Dog Repeller Device

This device is a cylindrical container of pressurized gas, capable of repelling a guard dog from a distance of six feet. The dog repeller comes packed in a hermetically sealed can for protection and concealment, and it is opened with a sardine key attached to the top.

To use the repeller, the protective cap must be removed from the cylinder and the side of the discharge valve must be pressed (the valve should be pointing slightly downward). A hissing sound will be heard as the gas discharges. The gas should be directed into the dog's face. One long burst should be more than sufficient to frighten the animal, but the action can be repeated if necessary.

The animal will incur no lasting injury, and it is extremely unlikely that it will return once sprayed. (The device may be used as a surprise gambit against humans as well, but be ready for follow-up action.) The very low temperature of the Freon-derivative spray causes burning and smarting of the eyes, which stuns and frightens the dog momentarily. (Tear gas was found to be ineffective against dogs; in most cases, they will continue to attack.)

Each device has a label indicating weight in grams and ounces. Prior to using on operations, the agent should ascertain the weight to determine the amount of leakage and gas remaining. If the cylinder is less than one-third full, it should be discarded (it should never be incinerated).

Drug capsules for doctoring hamburger meat fed to dogs, along with an antidote Syrette, may also be obtained from KURIOT. There is a dose-to-weight scale to be followed. CIA also provides a dog dart kit, complete with long-range attachment, that launches a dart drugged with a morphine derivative for knocking out guard dogs. An antidote also is provided.

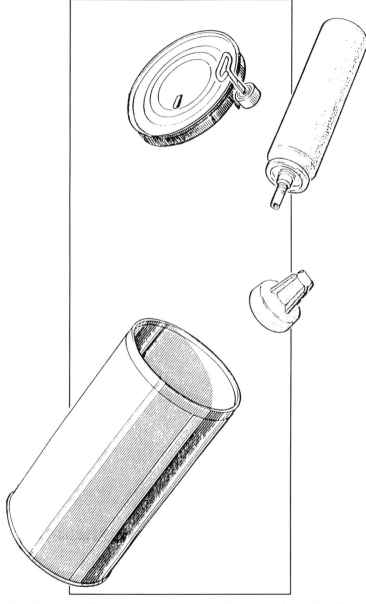

The dog repeller as it comes in the can. (CIA/author illustration.)

The dog repeller in action. (CIA/author illustration.)

Animals must be protected from exposure to the elements while unconscious. They wake up groggy, but none the worse for wear.

Item 9: Lapel Daggers

These diminutive daggers became popular as World War II hideout knives. They were typically short, double-edged blades, not unlike the final inches at the tip of a Fairbairn-Sykes commando dagger, and they had a vestigial hilt that was grasped between the thumb and forefinger.

The weapon often had a hole drilled through the grip, which had a knotted loop or cord through it. This loop, which was passed over the forefinger, prevented the blade from slipping backward during a thrust, saved it from being accidentally dropped, and generally made it more secure in the hand. The finger loop allowed the weapon to be hidden from sight, and yet the dagger could be swung around the finger as one would a key ring and be available instantly. In response to a command of "Hands up," the operative could swing the blade to the rear of upstretched, "empty" hands that seemingly posed no threat to an arresting officer.

Originally, the lapel dagger came with a leather sheath that had stitching holes on the back for sewing to the clothing. As the name implies, its typical location was under the lapel. In World War II, the Gestapo soon got into the habit of feeling behind the lapels of suspected agents, and the presence of a lapel dagger or "L" suicide pill on a stickpin was a dead giveaway. The weapon could be sewn into a pocket, up a sleeve, or inside a gaiter as well. One French Canadian SOE agent kept his under the collar behind his neck so that if he were ordered to put his hands up, he would be able to reach it quickly. He practiced throwing it at a dart board until he acquired great skill and accuracy.

The weapon is said to be derived from the Scottish "Skein Dhu," which was held by a garter under a knee stocking so the kilted warrior could reach for it when downed.

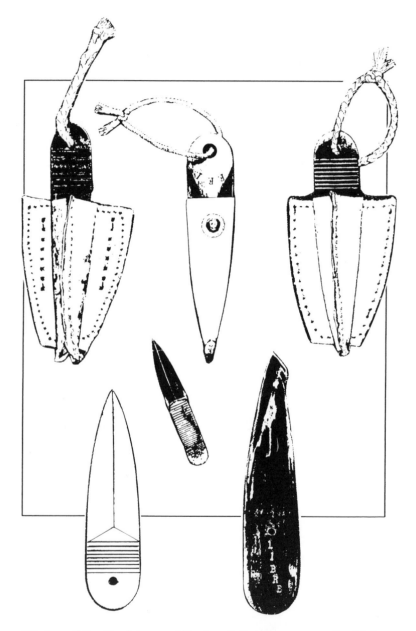

Blades of the Resistance. The lapel dagger was used widely in World War II. (Illustration courtesy of Keith Melton.)

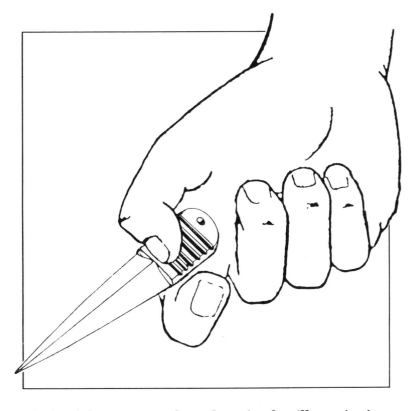

The lapel dagger grip is shown here. (Author illustration.)

Lapel daggers were also available commercially at British service uniform shops during World War II.

Item 10: E&E Suppository MK I

An attempt was made during World War II to provide a complete escape tool kit housed in a rubber capsule that could be carried internally if necessary. Pushed inside the anus, it could be held in place by the anal sphincter and would obviously pass all but the most intimate of searches. (This hiding place is nothing new; it has been used by prisoners and smugglers for centuries for stowing contraband. Prisoners use "le plan," as it is called in Europe, to secrete cash or illicit drugs inside custom-made aluminum or brass tubes with threaded caps. Daggers, and even guns, can be made to fit this profile as well.)

This kit contains a set of saw, file, and knife blades, as well as a drill and reamers. There is also a wire cutter with screwdriver and pry bar. With such an array of hardware, a prisoner could conceivably free himself or herself from shackles, make a key, disassemble a lock or door from its hinges, cut a barbed-wire fence, saw through a panel or bamboo floor, attack a guard, and even steal a vehicle. There are myriad options.

This compact kit is waterproof, of course, and while it would generally be carried in a pocket as a wallet, on operations in which one is in danger of being captured, it is stored where intended. Once one becomes acquainted with the item, it is not uncomfortable to carry; in some cases, it is a great comfort to know that it is always close at hand.

Modern search techniques and the popular x-ray scanners and metal detectors will uncover this device, but these do not come into play in a preliminary search, which is the time that the device may still be used. Psychologically, the prisoner may be down for being caught, but the most opportune time for escape is in the early stages of capture during transfers, while waiting in holding cells, during breaks between interrogations,

The Suppository MK I escape kit with assorted tools displayed. (Illustration courtesy of Keith Melton.)

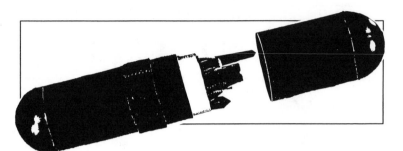

Suppository kit assembled into stowage capsule. (Illustration courtesy Keith Melton.)

and so on. The usefulness of this device depends upon the sophistication of the country of operation.

Item 11: E&E Suppository MK II

This escape kit contains an excellent take-down wire cutter with extending handles for increased leverage. The handles also accommodate an abrasive saw-edged knife, a file, and an X-ACTO-type blade. A drill bit is included as well.

The parts fit into a compact frame that is sealed in plastic. The device is shorter and flatter than the MK I, but some opine that it is not the best shape, as it is also thicker in a critical dimension. (Length is not as important as thickness when it comes down to a satisfactory fit.) Perhaps in light of this feature, a small plastic container of surgical lubricating jelly is issued along with the kit.

The shape does allow it to be concealed elsewhere on the person—taped under the arm or between the legs, for example. (Females have an extra option, of course.) The device is not much different in configuration from a Buxton-type key wallet. It may be palmed and passed along to another individual. It is also moisture sealed and waterproof, so after retrieval it can be hidden in a toilet bowl or buried underground, for example.

Once again, this suppository is not a match for modern detectors, but it fulfills the same purposes as the MK I, plus some. The knives give it offensive capability as well as a means to cut bindings and restraints, fashion spears or arrows, or carry out small-scale sabotage (tire slashing, gas tank holing, or telephone line cutting), any of which may assist in the escape. The tools might also provide a means of access to arms or larger tools, and thus, further means of escape.

The leverage action of the cutting jaws of the snips allow it to cut through varieties of modern razor wire and barbed tape. An abrasive saw with a Remington coating will cut most steels and saw through brick and glass.

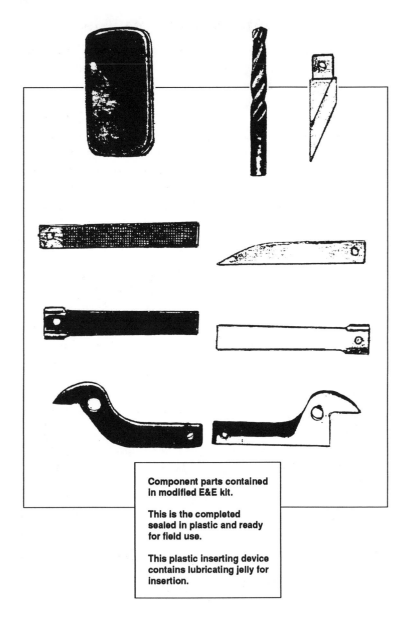

Component parts contained in modified E&E kit.

This is the completed sealed in plastic and ready for field use.

This plastic inserting device contains lubricating jelly for insertion.

The E&E Suppository MK II kit with assorted tools laid out. (CIA/author illustration.)

Item 12: Gigli Saw

The Gigli Saw is a bundle of specially braided tempered-steel wires that quickly cut through bone with rapid alternate pulling strokes, by means of finger rings at opposite ends of the wire.

Dr. Gigli was an Italian physician, and the device he invented in the early part of this century found much service in brain surgery, where the procedure required removing a section of skull to expose the brain. (The precise procedure was to drill four holes at the corners of the area to be exposed and then carefully introduce the Gigli Saw into one of these holes and feed it under

The surgical saw invented by Dr. Gigli. (CIA illustration.)

the skull above the dura mater. As it emerged through the next hole, it could be grasped and then attached to the finger ring. The sawing action would commence, cutting from the inside out, which made it a much safer procedure than using trepans or bone chisels.)

The usefulness of this saw as an escape aid was first noted by Clayton Hutton (Mr. X.), who designed escape devices for British MI9. He had it hidden in uniform linings, seams, and hatbands, but the most famous location was in the bootlaces. The bootlaces were hollow tubes, and it was simple to snake a Gigli Saw into them. The saw portion went through the eyelets, leaving enough lace to form the standard bow and knot.

As well as it could cut bone, the Gigli Saw was devastating on wood and could whip through a two-by-four in seconds. The saw's abrasive friction also worked on pipes and bars and, with proper technique, allowed it to cut through metal sheets such as galvanized iron. It was a prodigious escape tool.

The original Gigli Saw issued by CIA is still openly available through surgical supply houses and is of much higher quality than its later imitators. (It is not used in brain surgery to the same extent, however, since the advent of motorized abrasive cutters and laser technology.)

Item 13: Gigli-Saw Belt Buckle

CIA coiled the Gigli Saw into a very tight circumference that would allow it to be fitted into a hollow belt buckle. The belt buckle found use as a hiding place when it was observed that security staff who used metal-detector gates and frisk wands generally disregarded the metal response from the belt buckle, as most buckles tripped the sensors. This allowed a perfect opportunity to introduce the escape saw into any restricted environment. The device could also be hidden in a watch case or disguised as a key retriever.

The saw will cut through handcuffs or bindings. It can be used offensively as a cheese-cutter garrote to strangle (or, in fact, decapitate) by sawing through the neck and spine. In a POW camp, the saw may be fitted into a wooden bow frame and used as a tool. Attach it to an overhead spring-stick by using cord leaders, run it through a table, or affix it to a treadle slat and it will work like a jigsaw, cutting complex shapes to fashion more escape aids and props. With the use of dowel grips, it can cut through adjoining insulated and conduit sheathed wiring to cut power or cause shorts in alarms and electric fences. The ability to cut through natural gas and water pipes, joists, and thick

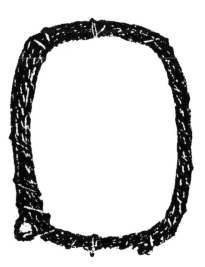

The Gigli Saw coiled to a size the could fit inside a hollow belt buckle. (CIA illustration.)

rope make it ideal for small-scale sabotage.

Left alone for a short time in a locked room, a captive could attack the floorboards, walls, or ceilings and circumvent the security at doors and windows. Once wormed behind and back through a barrier, this little demon cuts quickly and quietly and can make a manhole in short order. Prisoners on either side of a barrier could work in unison to cut through.

Outdoors, this device has come into its own as a survival tool in its reincarnation as the wire pacsaw (Item 31).

Item 14: Gigli-Saw Button

This button is also intended to pass through security checks, since metal buttons are usually disregarded in scanning. The button, which has a short length of Gigli Saw coiled within it, can be detached and hidden prior to an anticipated detention. The shape also allows it to be swallowed and then retrieved after it passes through the digestive tract. It may also be used as a suppository.

The location of the button on a coat or jacket is of importance. The best place on a bush- or safari-style jacket or any uniform with epaulettes is on the epaulette buttons. This enables one to bite the button off even when the hands are bound or cuffed. ("L" pills are hidden there, too, for the same reason.) A sleeve cuff is also an obvious location, because of its proximity to any wrist bindings. The button can be disguised elsewhere as a fashion accessory or sewn under the clothes, within a crotch pocket, and so on. The small size allows the button to be palmed easily or passed from mouth to mouth by kissing.

Apart from the Gigli Saw, there are other flexible, abrasive cutting devices. Commercially available Teflon strings and tape impregnated with abrasive grit for finishing metals will work their way through steel if a concentrated area is worked on; these can be rolled into a button as well. Prisoners in the United States will use toothpaste (as an abrasive) and dental floss, which they are permitted to ask for daily, to wear a cut in their prison bars over a period of time. Once, a police official at a

Shown here is a hollow button with a short piece of Gigli Saw concealed inside. (CIA illustration.)

detention center located on an upper floor of a high-rise police headquarters intimated to me that he knew this flossing activity was going on but wasn't concerned, as there was a hardened core to the prison bars that was impervious to such attack. Three men later escaped, one falling to his death when the sheet rope failed.

Item 15: Scroll-Saw
Temple Arm (Tube)

The concealment of a 3-in. length of spiral blade in stainless-steel tubing in the eyeglass temple piece offers the user a saw, gouging tool, and/or drill. Cutting rates: No. 8 steel fence wire, approx. 8 min.; 1/2-in. diameter col. rolled steel, approx. 15 min.

The temple arm is that part of the eyeglasses that extends backward along the temples and rests on top of and behind the ears. This sample of CIA issue stock is the popular steel-tube temple arm that attaches to steel-rimmed glasses.

Eyeglasses are the very soul of innocuousness and initiate no interest when they cause metal detectors to squeal. The reasons for wearing glasses might be prescription, reading, sun, driving, or safety. Non-prescription glasses are even used now for a fashion or "power" look. Glasses also aid in switching identities when being followed or assuming roles.

The arm tube houses a spiral saw blade of a family that includes the descriptions "fret," "scroll," and "coping," all of which are used for intricate pierced woodworking.

The blades are moderately flexible but will break if bent too far. Typically, a finely barbed surface progresses spirally along the blade. These barbs tend to cut wood with a clean, rasping action, and there is little

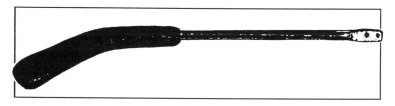

Scroll saw blade concealed in the steel tube of an eyeglass temple piece. (CIA illustration.)

tendency for the wood to split or crack from this type of cutting. Some craftsmen prefer a downstroke when cutting, while others prefer an upward cut for a more precise view and control over the advancing blade. Use as E&E devices implies that the saws will be hand-held, without a frame. They can be worked into cracks or chinks in wood structures and pulled back with a cutting stroke to gradually enlarge a breach. They are easily concealed in the hand and quickly dropped or eliminated if there is danger of being discovered using them. Although not made to cut steel, they can be pressed into service on an emergency basis. (Miniature jewelers' hacksaws do cut steel surprisingly well, however, and are a revelation to those who have never used them. The hollow temple-arm tube could house several saw blades, but a tensioned saw frame would have to be fashioned to get the best from a jewelers' saw.)

Item 16: Sabre-Saw Temple Arm

The sabre-saw blade is cemented firmly in the eyeglass bow, while the remaining part is concealed firmly in the temple piece. A dark plastic material must be used for the entire eyeglass temple piece. Blade is excellent for cutting wood.

The embedding of a sabre-saw blade into a plastic temple arm is consistent with the tapering width of both items. The blade is not visible when used on operations glasses, and plastic glasses are so common that they arouse no suspicion and blend well anywhere.

The sabre saw is a motorized reciprocating tool that uses various blades to perform different tasks. The blades are often interchangeable with jigsaw blades, which are more common. The sabre saw is capable of plunge-cutting through wood and other materials if the blade is first held nearly parallel with the surface and then gradually raised as the channel deepens and is finally penetrated. Once vertical, the saw can be guided into tight patterns, although it is not as handy as the jigsaw. This can also be accomplished, albeit at a far slower rate, by holding the blade alone in the fingers, giving the sabre saw an advantage over other escape saws that require a starting hole. The blades, which are fashioned of tempered spring steel, also have found use as hammer mainsprings for prison-made zip guns (which Special Operations E&E training covers,

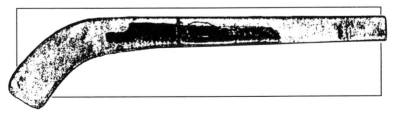

Sabre-saw blade concealed in a plastic eyeglass temple piece. (CIA illustration.)

depending upon the locale of the mission).

The temple arm must be broken open to get at the hidden sabre-saw blade. The blade is of the hacksaw pattern and will cut both steel and wood. Optional blades (carbide-coated, for example) that can cut ceramics, glass, and concrete are also available. The hacksaw blade is stiff enough to be used as is and can be grasped between the thumb and forefinger to cut deliberately through the intended medium. Simple handles may be fashioned to ease the task significantly. There are commercial handles available domestically that clamp to sabre-saw blades and turn them into handy keyhole saws. Miniature saw-blade holders made in the shape of pen housings have been recovered in prison shakedowns.

Item 17: Scroll-Saw
Temple Arm (Plastic)

A spiral saw blade which is excellent for cutting wood, steel, or plastic is concealed in the dark plastic temple piece. The eyeglass bow is cemented to one end of this saw blade. Cutting rate is similar to that of the tube scroll-saw temple arm (Item 15).

This eyeglass temple arm has the scroll or spiral saw fitted in translucent plastic and is very effective in that it is disguised as the strengthening wire found in the temple arms of regular eyeglass frames. (This feature is quite common in sunglasses and safety glasses as well.)

For emergency use, the plastic arm must be split open to get at the saw, but if the earpiece is left bonded, it forms a convenient offset grip for the blade. Some two-part designs allow the blade to be pulled out along with the earpiece so that it may be reinserted and the glasses still used. (The cracked joint is visible, however, and does make the glasses uncomfortable to wear.) As an added advantage, if the wrists are pinioned with flex cuffs, sash cord, commo wire, or the like, the earpiece can be held between the teeth and assist in cutting through the lashings. The bonded design is really the

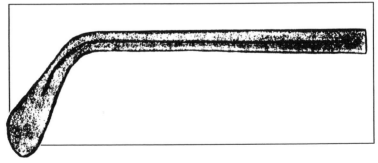

Saw blade concealed in plastic eyeglass temple piece. (CIA illustration.)

best for deep cover, and is so natural that the owner may get used to it and forget he or she has the escape aid at all, even when it may be of use! These blades always come in pairs (left and right) for consistency and balance, so there is always a spare one handy.

Those addicted to glasses with the temple arms joined by a neck cord have the advantage of another place to store a Gigli Saw, as well as a possible garrote. "Action glasses," which are often joined by a short elastic band to prevent them from falling off, are used by athletes and military personnel, for example. Their elastic strap is a less likely area for saw concealment, but could contain an abrasive Teflon ribbon.

The barbed spiral blade may also be used as a probe for fishing out messages from dead drops or as a broken key extractor (it can be positioned alongside a broken key and, when pulled backward, will dig into the key and extract it).

Item 18: Hacksaw-Blade Temple Arm

The width of a hacksaw is reduced by grinding to fit in the eyeglass temple piece. The hacksaw blade cuts through No. 8 steel fence wire in three minutes.

This two-part, opaque temple piece is a hacksaw contained scabbard-like within the long forepart of the temple arm, with the earpiece rear portion serving as an offset finger grip.

This hacksaw is capable of cutting through handcuffs and bindings. In some cases, just the center link would be attacked so as to initially free the hands, and the "bracelets" would be seen to later. If the hands are cuffed behind the back, it is sometimes possible to slip them down the back of the legs under the feet to bring them back in front, or if this cannot be achieved, to simply work on the cuffs behind the knees. Cutting with a hacksaw is tedious work, even under the best conditions, and these little blades are the "junior" hacksaws favored by plumbers for work in tight places. The forward stroke is the cutting stroke, and the pressure on the blade must be eased slightly on the reverse or drawback stroke so as not to wear the teeth unnecessarily. (With hacksaws, the points of the cutting

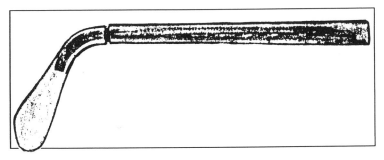

Hacksaw blade concealed in plastic eyeglass temple piece. (CIA illustration.)

teeth point forward, toward the work.) Regulation cuffs are chrome- or nickel-plated, and they will resist the hacksaw for a time, but once a start has been made the cutting will proceed a great deal faster. Efficient cutting requires concentration and blade control, and the operator must try to use as long a stroke as possible so that the maximum number of teeth per inch bear on the metal. The blade can be lubricated and its work quieted with saliva. In long-term confinement, the hacksaw can also be used to cut out and form larger pieces of metal, such as knives, arrows, or spear points. (Even the bevel of the blades can be roughed out with the hacksaw.) Specialist tools such as bar spreaders, custom gouges, or trowels might be made with the primary assistance of a hacksaw blade.

Bear in mind that not all incarceration is formal or sanctioned; witness the kidnappings of CIA personnel. A hostage with a hacksaw has an edge—a cutting edge.

Item 19: Dagger Temple Arm

This pair of glasses contains several blades and cutting weapons. The temple arms conceal two daggers, and the lenses act as cutting instruments that are ground sharply along the lower portion that rests within the frame. The tangs are embedded in the earpiece section, and the narrow daggers are nestled within the temple arms, replacing the reinforcing strip that is common in eyeglasses. The lenses can be prescription-type; in fact, this is preferable for ruse purposes.

The frame must be softened by heat or broken away to release the lenses. Glass may be honed to incredible sharpness, and the concave shape of eyeglass lenses allows them to be gripped easily. They are brittle, like any glass, but if they are ground from industrial safety glasses, they tend to hold up a lot better. The cutting edge may be used offensively (held against a throat, for

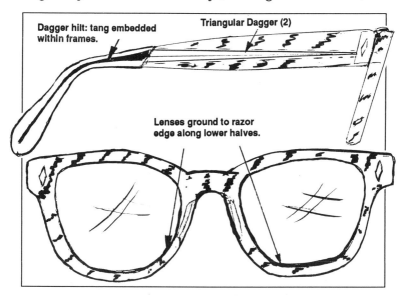

Dagger temple arm. (Author illustration.)

instance), but its primary use is to cut bindings. The blades are double-edged, made of hardened steel. They are flat and triangular at the cross section, with the spinelike apex adding some rigidity and strength. Although the dagger can cut and inflict slashes, it is intended as a one-time piercing weapon; hence, the desirability of the second backup dagger. These follow the pattern and use of assassination daggers, which are thrust home and then snapped off (leaving nothing to help the potential aid-giver determine what occurred and perhaps disguising the location of the wound long enough so that treatment will be ineffective).

These glasses have the ability to pass through metal monitoring checkpoints and even body searches, allowing the agent to be equipped with an escape aid that is overlooked because it's so transparent.

Glasses-case weapon, page right. First page of the actual instruction sheet provided for the Llama Pressin Pistol, which shoots special .22 Center-Fire ammo. (Courtesy of Llama-Gabilondo, Spain.)

Item 20: Glasses-Case Weapon, .22-Caliber

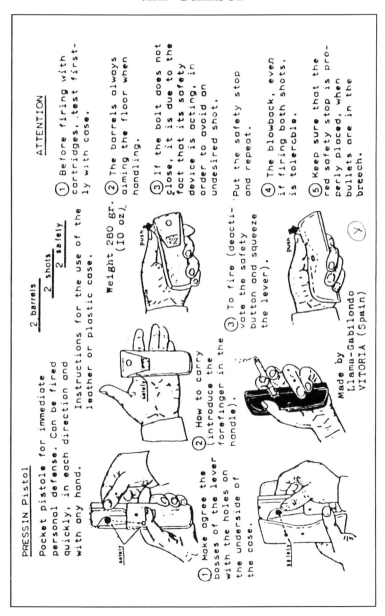

PRESSIN Pistol

Pocket pistole for immediate personal defense. Can be fired quickly, in each direction and with any hand.

2 barrels
2 shots
2 safely

Instructions for the use of the leather or plastic case.

Weight 280 gr. (IO oz)

① Make agree the bosses of the lever with the holes on the underside of the case.

② How to carry (introduce the forefinger in the handle).

③ To fire (deactivate the safety button and squeeze the lever).

Made by
Llamu-Gabilondo
VITORIA (Spain)

ATTENTION

① Before firing with cartridges, test firstly with case.

② The barrels always aiming the floor when handling.

③ If the bolt does not close, it is due to the fact that its safety device is acting, in order to avoid an undesired shot.

Put the safety stop and repeat.

④ The blowback, even if firing both shots, is tolerable.

⑤ Keep sure that the red safety stop is properly placed, when bullets are in the breech.

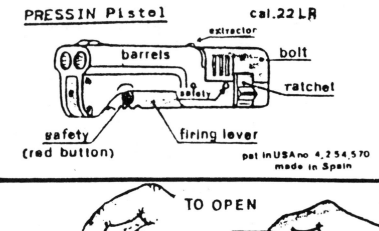

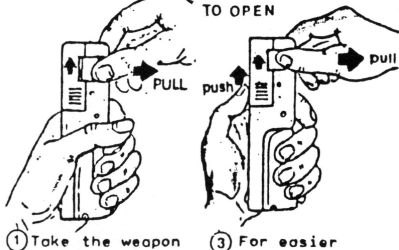

① Take the weapon with left hand, aiming the floor.

② To free bolt pull strongly the ratchet with two fingers of the other hand.

③ For easier opening actuate firing lever and then pull the ratchet and push the bolt.

Notice: To free the firing lever, open the bolt.

The second page of the instruction sheet for the glasses-case weapon is shown above and at right. (Courtesy of Llama-Gabilondo, Spain.)

With either hand, push lever.
(It can fire, either two almost simul-
taneous, or two shots independently).

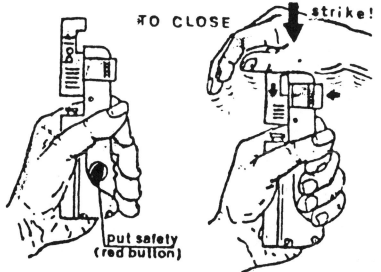

(1) Place red safety stop (MOST IMPORTANT)

(2) Load the weapon aiming the floor.

(3) Strike! the bolt with the palm of the hand.

(4) Fix the ratchet.

Test firstly with case.

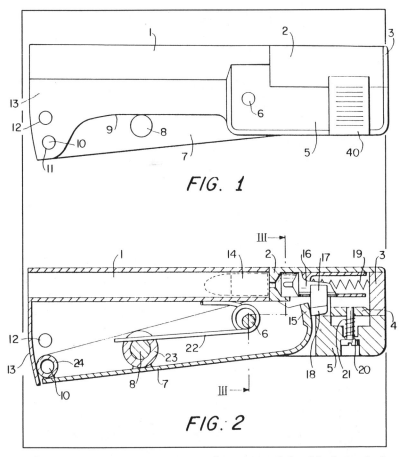

FIG. 1

FIG. 2

Glasses-case weapon. Patent drawing of double-barreled firearm invented by Juan Uriarte del Rio and Jose Jimenez-Alfaro. Note the short (part 17) and long (part 18) sears that trip in succession when lever (part 7) is depressed. (Illustration courtesy of U.S. Patent Office.)

Item 21: Hollow Belt Buckle

This metal belt-buckle assembly contains a miniature coping saw (see the belt-buckle saw, Item 22). This type of construction can be used for men's buckles in a variety of shapes and sizes.

This belt-buckle concealment device acts as a container for the miniature hacksaws and frames that follow. It is similar to the hollow belt buckle that hides the Gigli Saw (Item 13). The aim of both designs is to provide cover for the saws during a magnetometer sweep or metal-detector-wand frisk. These hollow belt buckles have an obvious advantage in that they do not have to be destroyed to access the saw.

The dimensions vary with the intended use, although it is obvious that the larger the buckle, the more space is available for an effective hacksaw blade. (Typically, a one-and-a-half-inch belt will require a two-inch buckle.)

Buckles shown here are for dress trousers and work clothes. Jeans may offer the ability to use larger belts and the more elaborate cowboy or trucker buckles, but these are often suspect, as they have been used in the past to hide derringers and knives. Buckles are also used on topcoats, mackintoshes, and luggage straps, all of which offer further options for concealment in transit, but might not be available if seized.

Hollow belt buckle with removable saw inside. (CIA illustration.)

Since official prisoners are habitually searched and their belts, laces, suspenders, and so on confiscated to prevent suicide, escape obviously must take place before processing reaches that point. (Such confiscation may not always be the practice in foreign lands and may not occur at all with radical hostage-takers, but as a general rule, immediate escape is ideal.)

Item 22: Belt-Buckle Saw (Pinned)

This unit was designed for insertion in the hollow belt buckle. The saw blade cuts through a 3/8-in. diameter steel rod in 20 min.; through a 5/32-in. concrete reinforcing wire in 15 min.; through a 1/4-in. diameter hardwood dowel in 45 seconds.

This miniature hacksaw and frame fits within the hollow belt buckle (Item 21). A length of "junior" hacksaw has small holes at each end through which pins are driven to secure it to the spring-steel frame. The frame's limbs are squeezed together prior to affixing the pins, which places tension on the blade once the pressure is released. This makes for straighter and more efficient cutting. The blades cut very well, considering their extremely limited stroke, and they will make quick time through a handcuff or shackle (literally flying through rope and nylon ties).

These hacksaw blades may also come encased in a flexible flat rubber strip (a British stratagem) that resembles a stick of Dentyne chewing gum in dimension and appearance. It may indeed be swallowed and later regurgitated or passed through the system. (The idea of swallowing escape aids may be traced back to the turn of the century, when the great escapist, Harry Houdini, witnessed a Japanese magic act in which the performers swallowed ivory eggs and balls and

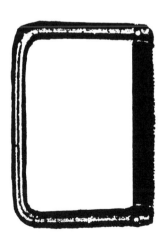

Saw that fits inside hollow belt buckle, with removable blade. (CIA illustration.)

regurgitated them at will. He studied and perfected their technique so that he could swallow and return similar objects; only for his purposes they were hollow and would contain a selection of picks and tools. In this way, he could pass a thorough nude search—having swallowed his escape eggs before coming to the prison—and then, by regurgitation, bring the tools up and go to work on the jail locks, of which he was thoroughly familiar.)

It is not expected that this degree of skill be attained by CIA agents, but it is within reason to expect that a rubberized blade might be swallowed and then recovered by using a soapy water emetic or applying a finger to the back of the throat. Drug smugglers often swallow prodigious amounts of contraband in condoms or balloons packaging to get past customs (and sometimes die when a package bursts). This is not likely to happen with the hacksaw blade's rubber sheathing.

Item 23: Belt-Buckle Saw (Slotted)

Miniature coping saw is exactly the same as the one used in the pinned belt-buckle saw (Item 22), except that a method for removal of worn-out blades has been incorporated in this model.

The slotted belt-buckle saw differs from the previous device only in the manner of mounting. The pins are already in the the blade prior to its being fitted into the frame. The frame is squeezed enough to allow the blade to be seated with the pins entering their slots. When pressure is released, the frame springs back, tensioning the blade. (To ascertain proper tension, one must pluck the blade like a guitar string. A high "ping" should be heard.) This is the mounting procedure used on coping saws and "junior" hacksaws, and it allows for dismounting the blade in the field. More importantly, it is an advantage in situations where the blade may be more easily handled inverted in the frame when cutting out of a handcuff, for example, rather than cutting in. (Double-sided hacksaw blades were tried for a time but were found to be more sensitive to breakage.)

Most handcuffs are made of iron or steel. Hardening, if it occurs at all, will occur in the surface plating or case, and this can be sawed

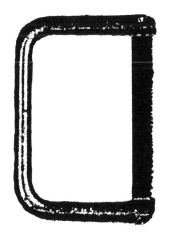

Saw that fits inside hollow belt buckle, with slotted frame for ease of blade removal. (CIA illustration.)

through with proper diligence. The Japanese Masuri brand is a popular import cuff made from chrome-plated brass.

Fine-toothed saws are quieter, easier to control, and often better for cutting harder steels. These little saws are deadly on flex cuffs, which are used as substitute restraints by police forces in large suspect roundups.

Aside: I once handcuffed a very powerful man with a flex-cuff-type restraint, whereupon he bent forward, pressed outward against his wrists using the base of his palms as a fulcrum and bearing surface, grunted, and stripped the ratchet-locking mechanism. I was later able to do it myself, but the pain was intense, and only the fact that I had seen it done allowed me to increase the force to a point where the restraint failed.

Belt-buckle hacksaws can also cut the exterior handle off a key-in-the-knob lockset to allow access to the mechanism and permit entry or escape.

Item 24: Belt-Buckle Saw (Integral)

This buckle was cut from a solid piece of aluminum and filed to shape. A removable side of the buckle has a slit which fits on the blade. Many methods of camouflage may be used to cover the slit that covers the blade. The cutting capacity of this device is similar to that of the pinned belt-buckle saw (Item 22).

Cast within this metal buckle is a saw blade. In such a form, it will pass the closest scrutiny, but this comes at the expense of not being as available for immediate use as some of the other models. The casting metal can be worn away by rubbing against any hard or roughened surface to expose the comparatively harder teeth of the saw. When exposed, the saw blade serves in a rasping or filing capacity initially, but as the casting metal is worn away during the grating process the saw blades take over as intended and can cut through bindings and handcuffs.

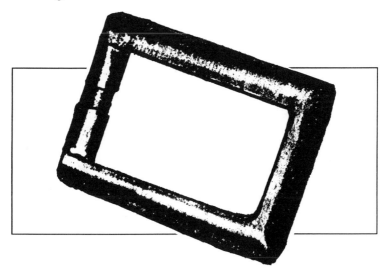

The saw blade is an integral part of this solid metal belt buckle. (CIA illustration.)

This metal belt buckle conforms to modern design for dress pants, allowing it to be worn with belts passing through narrower loops. The more discreet the buckle, the better its chance of passing an inspection without arousing any suspicion during a search or examination. (It should be noted that in the CIA belt-buckle saw models pictured here, the belt-notch fastener has been omitted for clarity. In operational use, the pin is wrapped about its axis in the normal fashion.)

Weighty buckles can serve as parrying weapons and flails when swung from their belts; they can hold their own against a group of attackers or a knife wielder. Soldiers have been known to sharpen the edges of their garrison belts for just such eventualities (not so much for combat against an enemy but for Stateside barroom brawling). This saw-edged buckle would serve admirably in similar circumstances. (The really wide buckles in fashion during the '60s, with the central notch-pin shaft, could also double as knuckle dusters: the four fingers encircling the notch-pin mounting shaft, with the pin projecting push-dagger-like between the second and third fingers; the big buckle itself resting flat against the knuckles and the first joints of the fingers; and the wide belt extending backward and wrapped around the wrist.)

Item 25: Saw-Edged Buckle (Embedded)

Cutting rate is low due to shortness of blade length. Cutting action is fair due to the permanently embedded saw blade. This item is effective in cutting metals of relatively small diameter.

In this model, the four saw blades face outward around the edge of the buckle and are embedded permanently into the epoxy-resin material that forms the body of the buckle. Here is another instance where current fashion may dictate what is to be worn on the mission. This buckle suits a style commonly used on women's clothing and is probably intended to be worn by women.

The blades are intended to act as rasps to quickly tear through bindings, but they would not be very effective against cuffs. It is often very hard to cuff

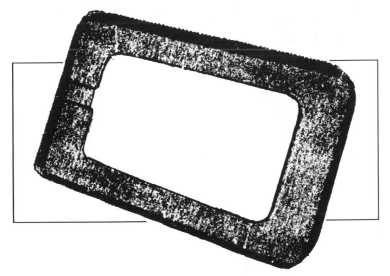

Epoxy resin buckle with pieces of several types of saw blades permanently embedded around the edge. (CIA illustration.)

women in any event, since their wrists are so small, the cuffs will not ratchet down to that size. Also, the relation between wrist diameter and hand width is such that they can often slip the cuffs off. (Harry Houdini was also adept in this technique when faced with "challenge" cuffs. He could flex his wrist muscles while being cuffed, convincing the administrator that he was secure by wincing at their tightness long before they actually were; then he would retire from view behind the curtains of his cabinet, whereupon he would relax his wrists, cover his hands with spittle for lubrication, attach the cuffs to a hook inside the cabinet, and physically pull the manacles over and off of his hand. Great pain and will power are associated with this stunt.)

The epoxy-resin buckle saw can cut through live wires with little danger, and this capability offers certain advantages for E&E (e.g., to switch off lights and alarm bells or cut into and bridge ignition-lock-switch wiring to start an escape vehicle).

Item 26: Buckle Saw (Molded)

This item contains three 1/2-in. blades and two 1-in. blades. Some difficulty may be experienced in using such short blades after removal from the buckle. Cutting rate, No. 8 fence wire, approx. 8 min.

The vinyl-plastisol buckle with short, spiral saw blades molded inside is suitable for use on men's and women's lightweight garments, such as bush jackets, raincoats, and dresses. There is too little ferrous content to register on any metal detector. The plastic is opaque, but even if the blades were discernible they would be dismissed as reinforcement framework.

The five short blades hidden within this design are removed by breaking away the plastic. The blades are barely viable as cutters, due to the short stroke they permit. They will work, but much patience is required, as are strong gripping fingertips.

The buckle itself is entirely vinyl, and its curved surfaces and edges allow it to be stored internally. Once released from the buckle, the wirelike saws are easily hidden about the body and could be readily twisted into the hair, beard, and so on, for later use.

These blades can cut through rattan and bamboo enclosures or be used to shape bamboo spears and other escape aids. Cutting

Vinyl-plastisol buckle with short saw blades molded inside. (CIA illustration.)

through steel would be difficult, but they could work through aluminum or brass. Bundled together, the blades can also be used as a compact rasp for shaping other woods.

These plastic buckles are a perfect cover. They are so common and inexpensive that they do not arouse much interest. The belts to which they are attached are usually made of cloth or plastic, so they will blend in with almost any disguise. They are even less obtrusive as part of a mackintosh, on which even a suddenly missing buckle will go unnoticed, since the belt is commonly knotted rather than buckled.

Item 27: Circular Saw Button

This item can abrade wood fairly well. The overall thickness of the device limits the cutting depth of the embedded tool. The item could be used to advantage in notching wood prior to sawing with other tools, such as abrasive coated saws.

This vinyl-plastisol button contains a small, circular saw blade. Outwardly, it appears quite common and blends in with a set of other buttons found on suit jackets, blazers, safari and work shirts, and so forth. Here again, the placement of the button can be rather strategic. Placement on epaulettes allows access to the button by mouth if the arms are immobilized. The coat cuffs are another option, as is the button fly. The button may also be swallowed or hidden as a suppository.

The plastic coating is cracked and broken away to reveal a cutoff saw of the type often used by hobbyists such as carvers and model makers. (Dremel Company offers a commercial version of this tool.) In regular use, the saw is affixed to the shaft of an arbor, which in turn is chucked into a high-speed, die-grinder-type motor or a miniature Unimat-type lathe. (Art imitated life in the James Bond movie *Live and Let Die*, where a motorized cutter was disguised as the elapsed time ring of a diver's wristwatch, used to cut through bindings.) The blades can cut off a variety of materials, such as wood, plastic, nonferrous metals, and steel. It is most unlikely that an escapee will have access to an arbor and motor, so it is intended as a hand-held device that cuts

Vinyl-plastisol button containing a small circular saw blade. (CIA illustration.)

by means of a linear scraping and filing action, advancing in a regulated fashion so as not to wear out the teeth. As with all hacksaws, it avoids exerting pressure on the reverse stroke. This is a tedious but sure way to cut through rope lashings or wire bonds.

The large variety of styles and shapes of buttons provides great opportunity to disguise E&E items of this nature. The clothes worn by an agent may be tailored to the situation.

Item 28: Circular Rasp Button

The cutting rate of this item is similar to that of the circular saw button (Item 27). It is possible to embed saws and other cutting tools in buttons in a manner such that half of the button can be removed easily, and then the other half acts as a holder.

This silicon, carbide-filled epoxy resin button is designed to function as an abrasive, rasp-like cutter. Additionally, it has short pieces of drill rod embedded into its matrix, which are arranged radially like the spokes of a wheel, giving structural support to the brittle carbide element. These drill-rod spokes, separated by a web of silicon carbide, give a cutting as well as an abrasive edge to this clandestine button. Carbide is one of the hardest materials, rating next to diamonds in that category. It is widely used in industry for grinding and cutting the toughest steels. It can easily

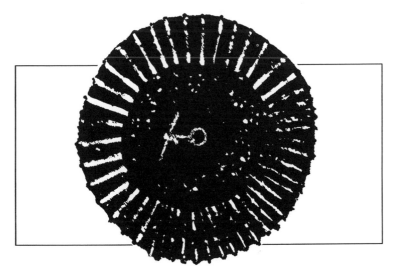

Silicon, carbide-filled epoxy resin button with short pieces of drill rod arranged like spokes of a wheel for an abrasive edge. (CIA illustration.)

score glass, so it may be used as a glass cutter for escape purposes as well.

Unlike the cutoff saw button shown previously, this tool can cut with a back-and-forth abrasive action. It will wear its way through any binding material, although care must be exercised not to twist it too much or it will snap. As a bonus, the drill rods serve as finger grips to help control the abrasive cutter. Using this cutter is still a tedious proposition, and an escapist must be patient while working.

Unless the button is coated with protective plastic, it should not be swallowed or hidden internally. It is, however, small and outwardly innocuous, so it can be palmed or hidden among personal effects. Uncoated or used as is, it resembles some real buttons, and it is certainly an effective disguise when used in conjunction with them. Of course, there is no limit to the number of escape buttons used on a garment; they could all be escape buttons if desired. It is always prudent to have a backup of several different escape items if at all possible.

Item 29: Scroll Saw Blades (3)

These spiral saw blades represent the best existing wire-type saws. Blades of this type may be used for sawing wood, steel, or other types of materials. When the end of the blade is sharpened, it becomes a fairly good drill. One disadvantage of the commercially available blades lies in their tendency to become less efficient with use. This type of blade is not very flexible and is difficult to conceal. Cutting rates: 1" x 1" yellow pine, 18 min.; 3/4" x 1" mahogany, 10 min.; 1/2-in. diameter aluminum rod, 5-1/2 min.; 1/2-in. diameter cold-rolled steel, 13 min.

Scroll or spiral saw blades are commercially available and come in various lengths to match the frame of the tool; the most common length is six inches. Many frames are adjustable, so that if a blade snaps, a long remnant may be mounted and used to continue sawing.

Since they are long, thin, and flexible, these blades may be hidden in a variety of places inside the clothing. The vertical seams of garments are a logical choice, but the blades also may be placed within hat brims for example, or be disguised as stiffeners for cloth visors. The canvas or cloth belt is another natural location for the blades, hidden under the surface, alongside seams, or within fashion welts and stitching. The curve of a belt is not sufficient to cause these saws to kink. (They should not be hidden in places that are likely to cause this.)

Their standard length allows the blades to be hidden in footwear, uniform gaiters, pant seams, fly flaps, pocket seams, forearm and upper arm seams, within dangling neckties, under collars, and behind lapels. They can easily be taped to the skin or hidden under bandages, wound dressings, or casts. They are easily snapped into more convenient lengths should conditions warrant it. The longer saw blades are easier to control with both hands and cut more efficiently.

It is necessary to shake or brush the blades from time to time while cutting wood, as they will clog with resin. Their spiral pattern makes them capable of cutting in either direction. The blades come in several grades and thicknesses, depending on their intended use. Some blades will cut aluminum and other nonferrous metals such as brass; it is possible to cut steel, but at the expense of rapid dulling. Rope, nylon, or wire bindings pose no problem for these saws, which will cut through wooden structures, including bamboo, with ease. In a POW setting, it might be possible to manufacture bow or tensioning frames for these saws, which will increase their efficiency tremendously.

At right are the three types of saw blades. (CIA illustration.)

Item 30: Belt-Buckle Compass

This concealment device utilizes a hollow latch pin on a sliding belt buckle. The buckle is of the pattern used on U.S. military service belts since World War II, but it has become so popular that it is seen in countries throughout the world.

Access to the concealment area is made by unscrewing a left-hand screw clockwise from the latch pin. This is the reverse of the standard unscrewing motion (i.e., counterclockwise), so as to forestall inquisitive searchers. (The same ruse was used with the end caps of World War II escape pens housing miniature compasses and silk maps.)

The latch pin on this buckle contains a small bar magnet and a thread, which together function as a compass when unraveled and held suspended. The bar magnet, being a permanent magnet, may be used to magnetize other items, such as sewing needles or razor blade slivers, which can be passed along to other escapees. The sewing needle will float on a piece of cork in a cup of water and point north-south, while the razor blade pieces can be trimmed to standard compass dimensions, mounted on a pivot, and housed neatly in a matchbox or plastic case.

The tubular latch pin may be used to conceal escape maps, complex instructions, or microfilm, for example. Miniature radio parts, such as a geranium diode, could be hidden inside and serve as the basis for a radio receiver to be constructed in prison camp. Inmates tuned to local events would know when to stage escapes. Similar small containers have aided POWs and escaping agents by housing concentrated dyes for altering uniforms, drugs for guards or wounded comrades, pep pills for increased endurance, tranquilizers for the noses of tracking dogs, and poison for the enemy or the agent.

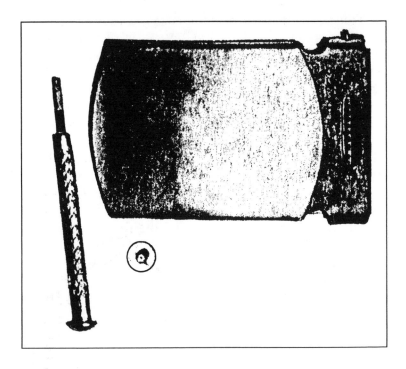

Hidden inside this buckle are a small bar magnet and thread, which together function as a compass. (CIA illustration.)

Item 31: Wire Pacsaw

The use of flexible or collapsible saws goes back to the trenches of World War I, where a rollup saw resembling the jointed saw chain of the modern power chainsaw was supplied along with two toggle grips. This saw was reissued to commandos and others in World War II. The Soviets supply a very efficient folding survival/escape saw resembling a large jackknife, which is easily stored in a pocket.

The Halland Wire Pacsaw used by CIA is the best commercially available wire saw. It is fairly flexible and will cut practically any type of material other than case-

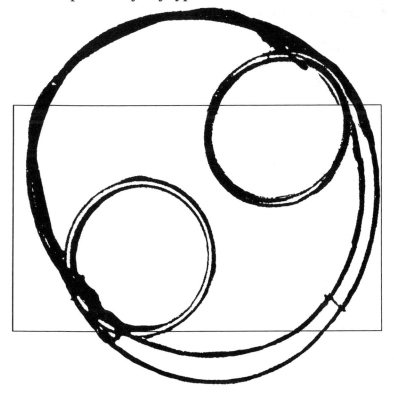

The Halland Wire Pacsaw is to be used for emergency camp or survival purposes. (CIA illustration.)

hardened steel. Care must be taken not to put more than a 45-degree set into the saw, otherwise the wire will break. The Halland Wire Pacsaw resembles the Gigli Saw in nearly all respects, except it is thicker and thus not as flexible, and the braiding is not as complex or as efficient as that of the Gigli Saw. It is intended as an emergency camp saw or survival saw. It is handy in that it could form the middle section of a weighted line thrown over a high tree branch (or rafter) and be worked to and fro from the ground. The saw has large key rings that form finger grips, but these are easily dispensed with when the saw is hidden inside a belt or hat brim. Wooden grips or pipe toggles could be made for the saw to allow for a stronger grip and greater control during an escape. The saw may effectively cut through frontier obstacles, such as wire stakes and wooden fence posts, and at least one source states that it can double as a garrote.

With all the Pacsaw's strong points and its availability from open sources, it is curious that CIA was not able to supply it more expediently than three to four months from the receipt of an order.

Item 32: Pencil/Belt-Buckle Drill

This device was developed to equip the operative with a drill and drill brace. The pencil contains the drill, which has an eighth-inch-square end that fits into the slot of the belt buckle. The agent can be anywhere in the world and use this device; the pencils found in that area can be modified to suit requirements. A regimental or similar insignia normally covers the belt-buckle slot. (A fifty-cent piece or similar knurled-edge coin could act as a drill brace and be used in place of this type of belt buckle.)

Twirling a drill around and around with the thumb and forefinger may seem like a useless exercise in today's high-tech world of espionage, but this finger-operated drill is capable of drilling into wood and plaster to form "spy holes." In one case, British counterespionage detectives (Special Branch) were interested in the activities of a group of subjects staying in a boarding hotel. They rented the adjacent room, drilled through their own plaster and lath and that of the next room, carefully stopping before piercing the wallpaper. Then they patiently scraped the rear area of the wallpaper clean and pushed a tiny needle through it. With the lights out and drapes drawn in their room, they were able to watch the activities of their neighbors projected upside down upon the opposite wall. They had created a room-sized pinhole camera.

The drill can also pierce sheet metal readily and could eventually cut an access hole into the case and mechanism of a lock in order to effect an escape. The cuff pivots of a handcuff could be cut away or a hole made to allow the depression of the star-wheel ratchet release.

It may seem tedious to the uninitiated, but finger-spun drills held in pin vises are used regularly in lock and clockmaking, and drills welded to "T" handles are

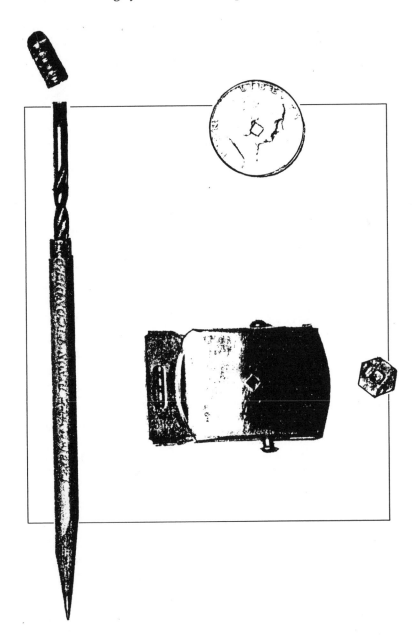

Pencil/belt-buckle drill. (CIA illustration.)

often used in industry as substitute reamers. As with any drilling, the sharper the tool the easier the work, and that applies doubly to this method.

Item 33: Dental Plate

This special dental plate serves as a rather expensive but excellent escape or concealment device. A small compass or a wire saw in a concealment tube is placed under a false tooth, and the scalloped front part of the plate can be used to saw, dig, or gouge. Each item must be custom-fitted for its user.

While the operative need not wear dentures to be fitted with a dental plate, it makes for a better disguise if he or she is already accustomed to wearing dentures.

Espionage history shows that senior Nazi officials successfully used false teeth to carry lethal poison during World War II in order to avoid capture or the hangman's noose. (The idea of carrying a lethal poison in the mouth may seem bizarre, but the rubber-coated British "L" pill could not be activated unless crushed in the mouth. It could be safely swallowed if not crushed,

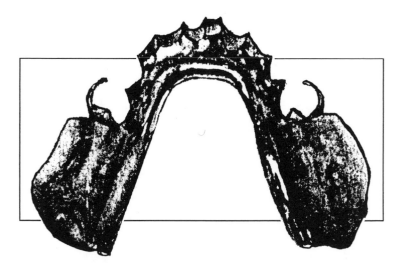

Dental plate. Stainless-steel cutting end (top). Platinum tubes for concealment (bottom left and right) are part of the plate's construction. (CIA illustration.)

and pass on through the system.) The dental poison pill could also be used offensively, being retrieved and placed in an enemy's food, for example. A similar stratagem, the use of poison lipstick (supposedly a development of the James Bond era), has been known in spy literature since the 1930s, and a razor blade clenched between the teeth is detailed in my *How To Kill* series (Vol. V), published by Paladin Press. A tiny, one-shot oral pistol has also been designed.

An agent in the World War II underground converted the midget components of a clandestine radio to be accommodated in his false teeth. Modern technology, it has been rumored, has allowed the manufacture of a true transceiver to be housed in a dental plate, with the audio transmitted by bone conduction. CIA makes use of false palates that alter the timbre and inflection of the voice, effectively disguising it when making telephone calls.

Item 34: Belt Knife

The Canon Company brass belt buckle neatly houses a steel folding bottle opener. The edges of the opener can be sharpened to form a knife edge. Even if the device is discovered, its very utility acts as a disguise; there is little that is threatening about a bottle opener. It is, however, a dandy escape knife.

Since the 1970s, the belt-buckle knife has become quite common. There are push daggers and half folders, as well as throwing stars; authorities are familiar with all of them. The Canon Company's product predates the other versions by nearly twenty years, and it will sail through a metal-detector-wand sweep with ease, where the others will not.

The ability to pierce cans is the ability to nibble through sheet steel. The sharpened point of the can opener is almost custom-made for gouging through

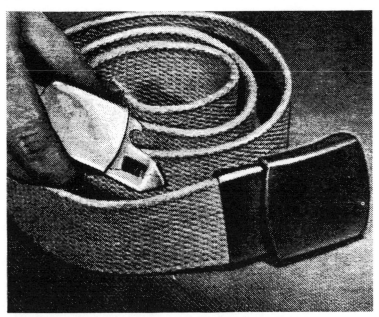

The belt knife. (Illustration courtesy of Canon Company.)

masonry joints. The leverage used to lift bottle caps can also be used to pry at and separate lock components or lift fence wire staples. The ability to cut and shape sheet metal also enables this tool to be used to make other dagger weapons and escape tools.

In parts of the world where the quality and quantity of water is questionable and the population is served by bottled water, the opener is an essential piece of military hardware. Israeli automatic weapons, for instance, have built-in bottle openers so soldiers won't be tempted to use a weapon's magazine lips as such. The Indonesian commando knife has an incongruous (to our eyes) bottle opener in the coil of the blade, because Indonesian servicemen drink bottled water instead of using canteens.

The belt knife has limited use as a weapon, although it is long and sharp enough to gouge the eyes or cut the throat of an opponent who has been captured. It might also find service swung from the end of the belt as a flail or scourge.

Item 35: Frisk Knife

The frisk knife was a British SOE weapon designed to be kept in a special sheath that was sewn to the inner side of a leather workbelt. This double-edged dagger is somewhat unique in that it was designed to fit the natural curve of the body. Its arc is such that when properly oriented the weapon can be nested against the small of the back, the radius of the hips and thighs, the curve of the shoulder, and so on. The weapon is so flat and the fit so close that it may defy a pat-down or frisk search.

This particular knife has a cord-wrapped grip that also forms a loop extension that enables the knife to dangle like a tail for a quick-draw advantage.

As an added boon, the downward curve of the frisk knife's blade compensates for the natural upward deflection a classic knife-fighting grip imparts (which normally would have to be adjusted for a between-the-ribs thrust). The advantages of this downward curve may be observed in the bent sword of the Spanish matador and occurred in later knives such as the original "bent-blade" model of the Gerber Fighting Knife, as well as one French foreign legion dagger that I happen to own.

An upturned, curved frisk knife in a different but similar application fits under the chin and against the throat particularly well prior to slicing. In a straightforward assassination attack, it is preferable that the wrist cord be used, because the lanyard prevents loss of a wet dagger and serves to stop the hand and fingers from sliding down onto the blade section during follow-up thrusts, once they are covered with blood. (For really deep cover, the cord grip and inner-belt sheath would be omitted, and the knife taped or stuck to the skin with surgical glue.)

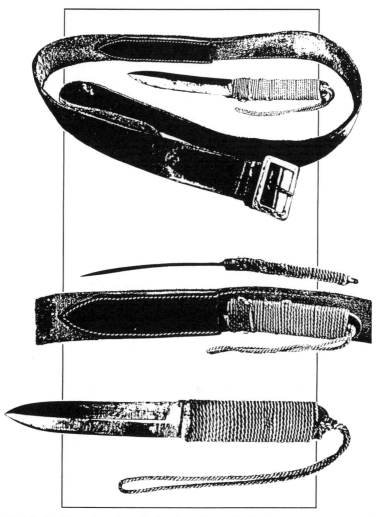

Frisk knife, showing belt sheath and distinct curvature of the blade. (Author/Keith Melton illustration.)

Item 36: Coin Knife

This miniature escape blade is riveted to an old English penny. Common pocket change is accounted for and disregarded by magnetometers, and scant attention is paid to it during search procedures. Even if discovered, it is likely to be dismissed as a novelty, and no nefarious intent need be explained. The choice of coin is purely arbitrary; any country's larger coinage could be used as a housing and grip. The blade may be extended or retracted by simply pushing or pressing with the fingers.

The coin knife was made in Britain during World War II based on suggestions from the underground. The gulletlike blade can be used as an aid to hook through ties and bindings prior to cutting. (This type of blade is a distinct feature on many French knives used for gutting, skinning, and pruning.)

The coin knife is quite safe to carry in the pocket; it is reminiscent of the knife blade issued to ditched aircrew for use in their rubber dinghies, because it wouldn't inadvertently sink the craft. The coin knife also served as a specific sabotage blade, used for slicing into the valve stems of the tires on Nazi vehicles. This was accomplished by trapping

Coin knife with gullet blade and pivot pin mounted on the head side. (Photo courtesy of Keith Melton.)

AAKRON RULE

Coin knife with alternate mounting of the cutter on the tail side. (Photo courtesy of Keith Melton.)

the stem between the rim of the coin and under the hooked blade. Pressing down with the thumb on the knurled portion at the back of the blade caused it to act as a cigar or pipe cutter, slicing the valve stem.

The knife has little value offensively. The gullet of the blade could be extended by grinding it to a claw point and then used to threaten the eyes or throat of a seized hostage.

The coin knife is small enough to be palmed easily. It could be ingestible (children swallow coins all the time). The blade is to be used when an operative is trussed up, functioning like the swing-out boot-heel knife to slash through bindings and cut by scissor action.

Item 37: Ring Knives

The ring knife is a contemporary of the coin knife and performs a similar function, being used to sabotage tires and to escape. It is, however, a more aggressive article, and being a ring, it can be hidden under the fingers within the palm and then swung around to become a knuckle duster and slashing weapon. Typically, the ring is worn on the forefinger and is supported in its slicing action by the thumb, which is pressed against the back of the hooked blade.

The origins of the finger-hook knife can be traced back to Africa, where it was used as a weapon by the Acholi tribe of Uganda. They wore their hook rings

A pair of ring knives with gullet cutter blades. (Photo courtesy of Keith Melton.)

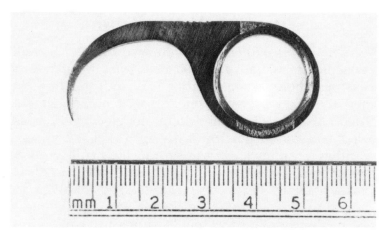

This ring knife has a distinctive hook blade. (Photo courtesy of Keith Melton.)

around the middle finger, with the blades curving out from the bottom of the fist.

Underground ring knives were made in Britain during World War II and were apparently all handmade, as no two are alike. Used as escape knives, they were well suited for cutting through ropes, cords, and tarpaulins. They fit the right forefinger, but they were slightly oversized to accommodate all fingers. Women or those with thin fingers could wear the ring over a bandage or glove for a snug fit.

The rings are small, flat objects, and while easily hidden, they are difficult to explain away if discovered. The talonlike hook could claw into the face or neck. (Carrying it openly on a key chain and calling it a pencil sharpener might be the best stratagem.)

There is a modern hook ring knife that is available commercially, made by Flash Manufactu Ring Co. of New Jersey. It is worn on the little finger and is used in the packaging trade for cutting strings and so on. On this tool, the blade extends from the ring in line with the finger. While it is small and handy, it is neither as flat nor as concealable as the underground rings.

Item 38: Insole Knife

The insole knives (there are two distinct models presented here) are concealed in sheaths stitched to or within a shoe's cushion insoles. The knives follow the curves of the instep for comfort as well as concealment. Both knives have dagger-pattern, double-edged blades, with a serrated portion midway down. There is a fishline wrist lanyard passing through a drilled hole in the pommel section of one dagger, while its counterpart has a hooked, gullet escape blade. These knives are from British World War II stocks and are quite unique.

In the '60s, custom-made shoes for concealing daggers were manufactured by the well-known firm of Wilkinson Sword and were commercially available from Tuczek's (London). Some modern shoes have a short length of formed steel in the construction of the arch, which can be removed, ground into the shape of a knife, and reinserted into the shoe. (Refer to the illustration labeled "The Arch of Triumph" in my book, *How to Kill, Vol. III*, published by Paladin Press.) Because this steel section is common, shoes fitted with the insole knife will pass through inspection even if the device registers on a metal detector.

The use of this type of curved-blade knife was discussed earlier in the frisk knife listing (Item 35). I once had two frisk knife sheaths sewn into the outer ankle portion of my boots, handles extending up under the trouser cuffs, and I practiced squatting, drawing, and throwing both knives simultaneously until I perfected the technique. The blunt pommel ends of the grips were sharpened like chisels and would cause wounds if the range was misjudged.

With this device, the option of using a pair of knives is always possible and perhaps necessary for a balanced gait, but the opposite shoe might also contain a further escape device, such as the insole gold (Item 39).

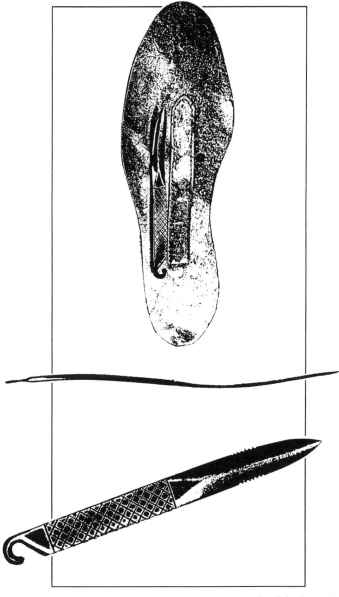

Insole knife with hook cutter. Note how the blade follows the opposite curves of the arch. (Author/Keith Melton illustration.)

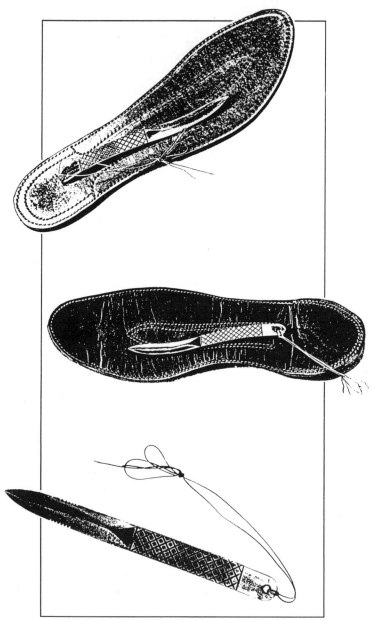

Standard insole knife with wrist cord. Note the serrated blade. (Author/Keith Melton illustration.)

Item 39: Insole Gold

The cushion insole is used for hiding away six British gold sovereigns. This SOE storage device is almost identical to that of the insole knife and was supplied by the same manufacturer.

One thing often overlooked in E&E lectures is the problem of finance. Money (or the things it can buy) is the basis of any modern escape. The prison systems of foreign lands are run from an entirely different perspective than in the United States. An imprisoned agent needs to be able to barter for improved conditions, if only to make the stay tolerable while trying to find a way to escape. Guards accept bribes as a means of supplementing their income, and all manner of contraband and perks can be bought at a price.

Likewise, agents on the run have to find transportation and lodging; people cannot always be expected to take them in and help them on good faith alone. In many countries, common folk simply could not afford to hide and feed an escapee, even if they wanted to. Their poverty is that abject.

Gold is a universal currency, and at four hundred dollars an ounce in 1989, it made eminent sense to stash several ounces as an escape fund. Third World black-market traders may take U.S. dollars, and credit cards might be useful, but both leave a trail and will break cover. Gold can discreetly buy an airline ticket, a month's lodging, a weapon, passage across a border, or, at the very least, the active cooperation of a disinterested third party. Sovereigns are small enough to be swallowed (the half dozen or more smuggled in the shoes represent a minimum escape reserve). If discovered, the gold merely represents a currency violation and may be unofficially confiscated, but the owner is not subject to the wrath of the police or investigation of authorities that would be inevitable should a special dagger be found.

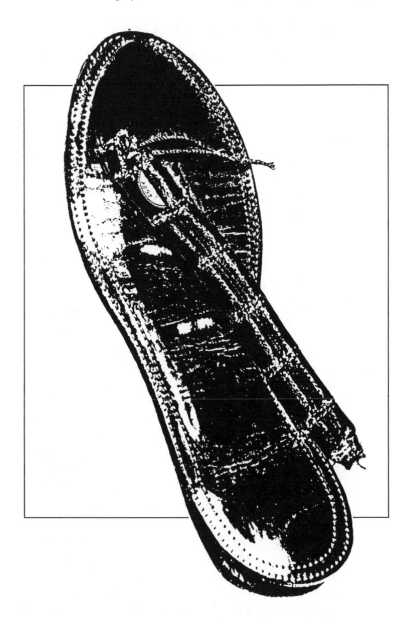

Insole with gold coin pouch. (Illustration courtesy of Keith Melton.)

Item 40: Belt-Buckle Gold

This belt buckle for modern dress trousers is based on a common gold-plated pattern. The leather belt is imitation alligator (and looks it), but the buckle is pure, 22-karat gold. It was issued as an E&E device to be used by agents as a source of emergency funds to buy their way to safety (at the very least, to a phone so that they

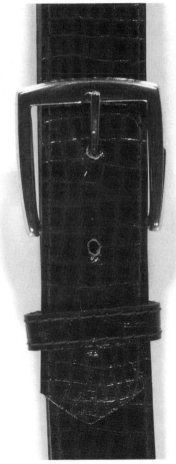

might notify CIA Control and arrange for a rescue). The belt buckle was to be divided up like the old Thalers into "pieces of eight" or "bits" and used as currency in the boondocks of the Third World.

The golden belt buckles were issued to CIA employees who served in Vietnam and became so de rigueur that they were almost a sign of recognition between agents —so much so that the practice of wearing them was done away with at the end of that conflict. The items were not considered expendable, but it is doubtful that many were returned. (A former CIA career officer of my acquaintance still wears his with as much pride

The golden belt buckle. (Author photo.) as any vet displaying his service medals.)

Being solid gold the buckles are heavy and would serve in some capacity as a flail in a fight and are capable of causing injury. Because it looks like gold plate, the buckle was worn in plain view and disguised by its inexpensive appearance, which elicited no interest.

The belts sometimes had a zipper sewn into the inner leather, creating a narrow money belt that allowed some cash to be hidden, safe from the predations of Saigon's infamous scooter-borne pickpockets. Ostentation in any form is always an enemy of the covert, so the wearing of gold rings, bracelets, and neck chains is always frowned upon. But even agents have to keep their pants up, and the belt buckle is a perfect cover for an emergency escape account.

Item 41: Rolex Watch

The Rolex has become one of the ultimate symbols of wealth and power. This is especially true in Asia, where a man is judged by the value of his wristwatch, and the simple elegance of the watch confers upon its owner the mantle of financial respectability. CIA officers with Timexes and Bulovas just couldn't cut it in this area when dealing with the moneyed generals and corrupt politicians of the Far East. The gold Rolex became the watch of choice for CIA personnel serving in Vietnam, and because of its distinction it was more high-profile than the gold belt buckle. It became a CIA trademark, and everybody knew it. (It reached

The golden Rolex. Note that the watch on the left has diamonds around its face. (Author illustration.)

ludicrous proportions. Upon arriving in Saigon, the CIA covert warrior would give the taxi driver the address of the reception house, and the driver would raise his thumb and yell over the traffic's din, "CIA, number fucking one!" Even in Washington, D.C., at a CIA training center known as the "Blue U," student officers using public transit to attend had to employ proper tradecraft to avoid "blowing" themselves or the school. When the bus pulled up at that corner and the students were rising to leave, the driver would gleefully announce to the passengers, "CIA men, this stop!" At which point, they would shrink back into their seats and proceed a couple of stops further along.) Contract employees sitting in hotel lounges in Bangkok and Singapore, as well as Special Forces types and Air America crews seconded to the agency, all sported Rolexes and yet strove to maintain their cover. Eventually, the watch became very popular with oil men, civilian contractors, and Walter Mitty agents—so much so that dilution served to blur the distinction.

Aside from being a symbol and trademark, the gold Rolex could be used to finance escape and assist an agent on the run, because it could be disbursed link by link. The Rolex Oyster Perpetual Chronometer: Don't Leave Home Without It.

Item 42: Comb Hide

Since a comb is likely to be found among the personal effects of anyone interested in good grooming, it has not been overlooked by those charged with finding places to hide E&E devices. Combs may be tucked into a pocket or held in the hand; since combing the hair in an open manner may be dismissed as an habitual affectation, it draws little attention from observers.

This commercial model has two compartments, exposed by drawing back on the two housings that slide along rails on the main body of the comb. The comb is made of opaque nylon plastic, and the compartments can store a variety of escape equipment, such as spiral saw blades, pills, magnesium ribbon, matches, .22 ammo, and so forth. (This sliding-breech design would be suitable for customizing into an aluminum or alloy comb to be used as a stinger item and actually fire a .22 round.) The device is not limited to this configuration and might be constructed with one long compartment that could hold a narrow dagger or lock pick. There is a commercial comb weapon, "The Defender," which drops (by gravity) a four-inch needle/dagger from its spine section with a thumb-button clutch release

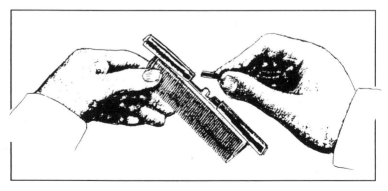

Filling the comb hide. (Author illustration.)

similar to that found on a drafting pencil. There is also a small combination comb/knife available that resembles the lapel dagger (Item 9) in size and application. It has a thumb grip (a small section of the comb used ostensibly to style mustaches). It comes with a little leather case that conceals the blade. The styling combs with the tapering handles could house hacksaw blades in the manner of the hacksaw-blade temple arm (Item 18). As long as they're nylon, they are not likely to be seized during an arrest. Because of the comb's traditional location in the back pocket, it is ideally suited for escaping from cuffs or bindings.

Item 43: Caltrop

The caltrop (calx = heel; trappa = trap: heeltrap) has been used for centuries as a military weapon. It is broadly equivalent in application to the ground-spike pistol and the "toe popper" land mine. Traditionally, the caltrop was an iron ball with four spikes around it so that whichever way it was placed, one spike was always projecting upward. (Punji stakes and the ancient Stimuli or planted darts are close cousins.) While the device could be used to deny access to foot soldiers, they could often pick their way through. It was especially useful against cavalry, which couldn't. During World War II, the U.S. Army Air Corps sprinkled caltrops on enemy runways; there was even a tubular type that would deflate self-sealing tires. Those caught in possession of such devices faced an immediate death sentence. A two-part, takedown caltrop was issued by the British to clandestine groups for sabotage and for thwarting pursuers. Both parts of this device were identical triangles, with the points

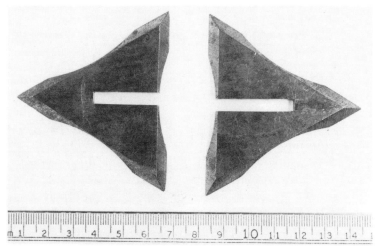

The takedown caltrop after being taken apart. (Photo courtesy of Keith Melton.)

AAKRON RULE

Overhead view of the assembled caltrop. (Photo courtesy of Keith Melton.)

ground to form blades and an assembly slot which permitted the nested pair to always stand with a blade pointing up.

While modern caltrops are almost always applied against vehicles, they do have other uses. A quantity of them can easily be carried disassembled in the pockets. Agents on the run can set several around themselves while they sleep. The blades are sharp enough to cut through bindings and may also be used as gouges to chisel through wood and scrape away mortar. The caltrop halves may be thrown individually in the manner of Japanese shuriken, which are thrown at right angles, like

World War II sabotage caltrops. The "Christmas tree" (left) and the "upholstery tack" with lead in cup (right). (Photo courtesy of U.S. Army Air Force.)

a frisbee. The caltrop's configuration also permits it to be used as an arrowhead or spear point.

Disguising caltrops can be difficult, partly because there must generally be a lot of them to be effective. An escape set of two halves might be arranged to form a star motif for a belt buckle and held in place by a central boss or threaded stud.

Item 44: Screwdriver and File

This prototype combination screwdriver, file, and drill brace has been fabricated from the finest file stock. The hole in the center of the brace is an eighth-inch square and works with the drill of the pencil drill (Item 32) for attacking locks. The whole set is approximately the size of a U.S. quarter dollar and was designed for concealment (within a plastic wrapper or condom sheath, it might be hidden rectally). The item is easily palmed or disposed of. It should never be swallowed, but it could be popped into the mouth temporarily.

The screwdriver resembles the key chain screwdriver medallion made by Colt Firearms. Looping a key chain through the center hole of this device would allow it to be kept in plain sight and be dismissed as a harmless souvenir. The screwdriver blade can also be used to pry and gouge.

Being made from file stock, the tool can be used for filing through cuffs or abrading ties and bindings. It might also be of assistance in making keys and picks, sharpening blades and saws, or fashioning drills in a POW setting. Permanently magnetizing it might appear counterproductive on the filing side but would help in making a compass and also serve to keep it hidden from detection when attached to

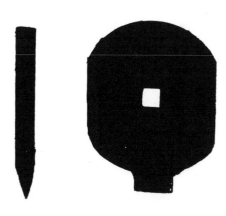

Combination file and screwdriver. This is the prototype constructed from a machinist's file. The center hole can be used as a drill brace. (CIA illustration.)

obscure metal surfaces.

On the run, it can be used to notch and break fence wire; score window glass prior to breaking; sharpen handmade wire fishhooks, arrows, and spear points; and in really primitive situations, strike sparks from flint to start a fire.

With the drill attached and the brace held in the base of a cloth-cushioned palm, this device could serve as a dagger. With the downward smash of two cupped hands, an agent could penetrate the skull of a seated enemy.

Item 45: Throwing Frisk Knife

The design of this knife is similar to those manufactured in West Germany and Japan for throwing purposes. This item is very thin and well balanced, and so may be concealed readily on a person's body. The hiding places are similar to those for the frisk knife (Item 35).

It will come as a surprise to collectors of combat knives that CIA has selected one of the most commonly available throwing knives as its dagger of choice. The knife is disdained by "experts" and generally sells in sports and novelty stores for about three U.S. dollars. These knives can be purchased as a set of three (one red, one white, and one blue), complete with a white plastic sheath or a wide, pancake-like pigskin leather sheath, either of which would fit a back pocket handily.

The throwing frisk knife is gripped by either the blade or handle and pitched like a baseball as hard, fast, and accurately as possible. If it has stuck, the agent must immediately charge after the knife and drive it home. If it

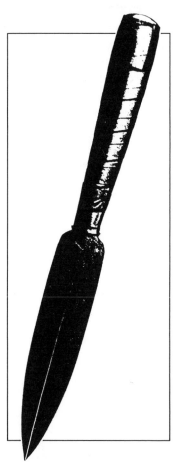

This frisk knife is designed for throwing. It can be concealed easily on the body. (CIA illustration.)

merely shocks by impact or misses, the agent must scoop it up and continue to attack. In this scenario, throwing must be considered an opening gambit, not an end game. For assassination purposes, this knife is so thin that it can be driven into an enemy well past the hilt and might even be thrust completely under the skin by continuing with a palm shove. In survival situations, the blade could be lashed to a pole, making an effective pike or spear.

(For details on a survival flare pen gun/frisk knife combination weapon design, see my book, *Fingertip Firepower: Pen Guns, Knives, and Bombs*, published by Paladin Press.)

Item 46. Belt-Buckle Pillbox

This is the corollary of the belt buckle compass (Item 30). What appears to be the belt-buckle roller is actually a storage tube capable of holding five tablets in a spring-loaded drawer. This item is commercially available from Health Safe Inc.; it was designed as a medicine dispenser for heart patients. The device is well made and unobtrusive, yet readily available. It would draw little attention even if discovered; its lifesaving capability need only be mentioned to allay suspicion.

This model fits a standard one-inch leather belt and is capable of holding the magnet compass device, a folded (bent over) lock pick or piece of Gigli Saw, lethal "L" pills, endurance stimulants (for escape), or any other variety of drug in tablet form.

A .22 cartridge or gunpowder compressed into pill form may be stored in the buckle along with primers and used as a starting point for constructing a simple zip gun. If desperate measures are required, the powder can be crammed

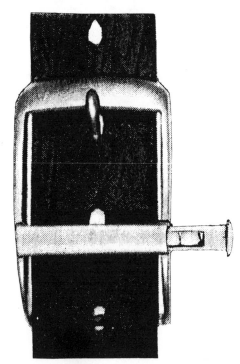

Belt-buckle pillbox. Note the tubular drawer extended to reveal two pills. (Photo courtesy of Health Safe.)

into the keyhole and touched off with a cigarette to create enough pressure to delaminate a handcuff lock. (Flash burns and minor wounds are to be expected if this course is followed.) It may also be possible to secrete a standard-pattern handcuff key within the storage tube (cut down and with the bow removed), and then bend the shank over to turn it. (There is a magician's gold-plated handcuff key available that can be worn like a lapel button or tie tack. The key has a pin soldered halfway down the shank and is held in place by a stud on the reverse side. It can also be pinned to the inner lining of coats and jackets; perhaps the best place would be at the rear, under the jacket tail.)

The belt-buckle pillbox could be expanded to apply to wider fashion belts or workbelts, allowing for even more storage room.

Item 47: Felt-Tip Blister Weapon

This blister weapon (or Vesicular Ointment Applicator MK III) consists of a felt-tip wick/applicator and a sealed ointment reservoir (it actually resembles a colorless oil and is available in limited quantities from KURIOT). The weapon is a little more than three inches long and may be carried in a pocket. It is designed for the surreptitious application of a blister forming (vesicular) ointment to items that will be handled by a specific individual. Any skin area contacted will be covered in blisters and mordant tissue in twenty-four hours. Depending upon the degree of exposure, the appearance and intensity of effects may vary. Blistering will heal within one week.

The applicator will remain inert until activated by pressing the felt tip against a solid surface until the wick breaks through the ointment reservoir seal. It takes approximately one minute for the blistering ointment to

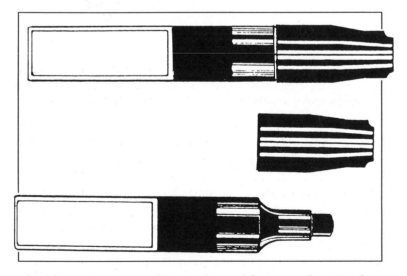

The blister weapon is disguised as a felt-tip marker. (Author illustration.)

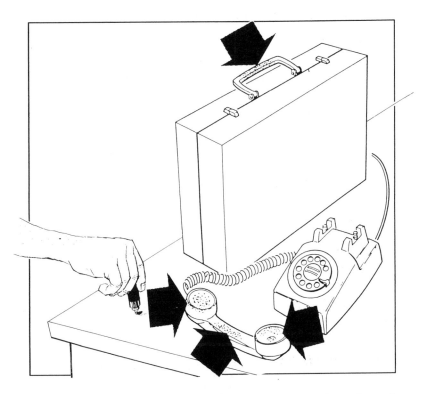

The blister weapon in action. Here, the weapon is activated by pressing it against the surface of a table. Arrows indicate possible areas for employment. (Author/CIA illustration.)

saturate the applicator.

To apply the blistering agent, the cap is removed, the container is held by the base, and the marker wick is held over the surfaces to be contaminated. Only a thin coating need be applied. There is enough material to cover seventy square inches effectively. The ointment will penetrate clothing and shoes, and not only will it blister the skin, it will cause blindness if it comes into contact with the eyes. (In the event of accidental exposure, the affected area must be washed immediately with an equal mixture of water and

Chlorox, Purex, or another 5-percent sodium hypochlorite (bleach) solution, and rinsed thoroughly.

This chemical weapon (mustard gas or chlorethyl sulfide) was developed under the aegis of a CIA project undertaken by the TSD (MKULTRA, 1954/MKSEARCH, 1963). Its brief was to "develop, test, and evaluate capabilities in the covert use of chemical, biological, and radioactive (CBR) material systems and techniques for producing predictable human behavior and/or physiological changes in support of highly sensitive operational requirements."

Item 48: Itch-Floc Disseminator

The itch-floc disseminator is a cylindrical metal device. It is three-quarters of an inch in diameter and comes in various lengths (eight, ten, or twelve inches). It contains a cartridge of compressed gas and a quantity of itching floc.

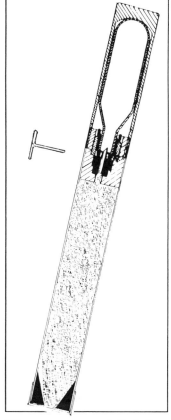

The gas-powered itch-floc disseminator, or "itchy gun." Shown here are the CO_2 gas cartridge, itch-floc agent, and safety pin. (Author illustration.)

When the device is fired, the plastic cap on the end is blown off and the itching material is dispersed by the compressed gas. The itching floc is disseminated in a cloud that will effectively cover an area of approximately four hundred square feet in still air. (Air currents from air condi-tioners, fans, and so on will increase the area covered considerably.)

The device is used for contaminating unoccupied indoor areas, such as conference rooms, assembly halls, and offices prior to a meeting. The material will cause an epidemic of itching and irritation when a room is later occupied.

To prepare the itch-floc disseminator for use, the safety pin must be removed by pulling the red tape located approximately two inches from the end of the cylinder to allow the cap to be blown off. To fire the disseminator, the device must be held at an angle of 30 to 45 degrees and the back section must be screwed onto the front section. This must be done with a rapid clockwise motion in order to achieve a quick release of the compressed gas and maximum dissemination of the itch floc.

The device should not be fired into a wind or draft, as the itch floc will be blown back onto the operator. The operator should leave the area immediately after firing the device to avoid exposure to the irritant. In case of accidental self-contamination, the operator should wash with soap and water as soon as possible. A local anesthetic applied to the irritated areas will relieve the itching. (A plastic bottle containing a first-aid spray is provided with the itch-floc disseminator.) No permanent physical damage or injury will result from exposure to the itch floc.